THE AMERICAN REVOLUTION
CHRONICLE OF AMERICA'S WARS

Lisa Frederiksen Bohannon

LERNER PUBLICATIONS COMPANY
MINNEAPOLIS

CHAPTER PHOTO CAPTIONS

Introduction: Early in the morning on December 26, 1776, Washington and his Patriot troops crossed the frozen Delaware River to attack enemy forces in Trenton, New Jersey.

Chapter 1: British troops storm the French Fort Ticonderoga in 1759, during the French and Indian War.

Chapter 2: An American minuteman (volunteer soldier) gathers his musket (gun) and equipment to meet the British in battle.

Chapter 3: Patriot Ethan Allen demands the surrender of Fort Ticonderoga from its British commander, who has just been roused out of bed, on May 10, 1775.

Chapter 4: Troops from Delaware march off to fight the British.

Chapter 5: American and Hessian forces engage in deadly hand-to-hand combat at the Battle of Bennington, August 16, 1777.

Chapter 6: Washington and Lafayette stand alongside their freezing troops at Valley Forge, Pennsylvania, during the winter of 1777–1778.

Chapter 7: American general Benedict Arnold (*right*) plots treason with a British officer.

Lerner Publications Company
A division of Lerner Publishing Group
241 First Avenue North
Minneapolis, MN 55401

Website address: www.lernerbooks.com

Library of Congress Cataloging-in-Publication Data

Bohannon, Lisa Frederiksen.
   The American Revolution / by Lisa Frederiksen Bohannon.
     p.   cm. — (Chronicle of America's wars)
   Summary: Chronicles the American Revolution, including the causes, strategies, and characters of the war, both famous and lesser-known.
   Includes bibliographical references and index.
   ISBN: 0–8225–4717–1 (lib. bdg. : alk. paper)
   1. United States—History—Revolution, 1775–1783—Juvenile literature. [1. United States—History—Revolution, 1775–1783.] I. Title. II. Series.
E208.B685 2004
973.3—dc21
                                                  2002010036

Manufactured in the United States of America
1 2 3 4 5 6 – JR – 09 08 07 06 05 04

TABLE OF CONTENTS

INTRODUCTION

Trenton, New Jersey. December 26, 1776. 4:00 A.M. The officers spread the password to their troops: victory or death.

For General George Washington and his army, the situation is desperate. The American Revolution, barely eighteen months old, has nearly collapsed under the force of the world's most powerful army and navy. Fewer than six months ago, in July 1776, the Continental Congress had declared America's independence from Great Britain. But this joyous occasion had been followed by months of miserable defeats and retreats, as King George III's troops had routed the Continental Army in one battle after another.

America's largest city, New York, had been captured months earlier. Since then, the British had been chasing Washington's army through New Jersey and across the Delaware River into Pennsylvania. Along the way, thousands of American soldiers had been killed, wounded, or captured. Thousands more had given up on the revolution and deserted, returning to their homes and farms. The Continental Army, which had numbered some nineteen thousand men in August, had dwindled to about five thousand ragged and weary troops.

Worse yet for Washington, the dreaded day of January 1 was approaching fast. On New Year's Day, most of his troops' enlistments—agreements to serve for a

certain period of time—would expire. These men would no longer be required to stay in the army and could return home. Considering their miserable situation, it seemed unlikely that many, if any, of these battle-weary men would want to reenlist and continue the fight. Washington's army threatened to all but disappear.

Weeks earlier, camped on the Pennsylvania side of the Delaware River, Washington had designed a bold and risky plan. Finally, on the evening of Christmas Day, 1776, the general and his men had marched to the banks of the Delaware. In near total darkness, as wind and sleet slashed their skin, Washington and his ragged army had transported cannons and equipment across the ice-choked river to New Jersey. Their mission: a surprise attack on the enemy camp in Trenton, nineteen miles away.

As the soldiers unloaded the boats on the New Jersey banks, the situation could hardly have been worse. Only about one-third of the invasion force had managed the crossing. Thousands had been turned back by the thick ice. The crossing had taken far too long. It would be daylight before the troops reached Trenton. The crucial element of surprise would be lost.

Most of the soldiers were dressed only in threadbare clothes. Many did not have shoes but had to wrap their feet in rags to try to shield them from the icy ground. With the words "victory or death" on their lips, the American soldiers marched toward Trenton, their cold and blistered feet leaving behind bloody footprints. With a victory, Washington hoped the spirits of his troops might be lifted, inspiring them to fight on. But should Washington's daring plan fail, the revolution—and the idea of America as a free and independent nation—might be dead.

THE RISE
1 OF THE PATRIOTS

Like most wars, the American Revolution was not sparked by any single event. Instead, the relationship between America and Britain soured over a period of several years. Most historians trace the roots of the revolution to the French and Indian War, which ended in 1763. Circumstances revolving around the end of that conflict brought about major changes in the relationship between America and Britain.

Before that time, Britain and its American colonies had lived more or less in harmony. Brisk and profitable trade with Britain, the West Indies (islands in the Caribbean Sea), and other European nations kept America growing and thriving. A key element in the colonies' prosperity was Britain's laissez-faire, or hands-off, approach to governing America. With some exceptions, Americans were allowed to do as they pleased—as long as the colonies remained profitable for Britain.

British subjects in America enjoyed more freedom than their counterparts in Britain. Only 15 percent of white males in

THE AMERICAN POPULATION

In the 1700s, the colonies' plentiful food supply meant many Americans ate better than their counterparts in Britain. As a result, people in America were, on average, three to three-and-a-half inches taller than people in Britain.

FAST FACT

Trade between Britain & America

The American colonies provided lumber for British ships, as well as tobacco, wool, furs, and sugar. In exchange, the British provided the colonies with manufactured goods.

British trade laws were designed to benefit Britain—sometimes at the expense of the colonies. The Navigation Acts, a series of laws passed between 1651 and 1673, allowed only British or colonial ships to trade with the colonies. In addition, any goods being exported from the colonies to other countries were required to pass through Britain, where they were taxed.

The Navigation Acts were often ignored by the colonists. Avoiding British customs taxes became a way of life for many American merchants. Smuggling became big business.

Americans did not have a completely representative government, however. In most colonies, royal governors had nearly complete authority. These men were appointed by the king of Great Britain and performed most executive duties. They signed laws, commanded the colony's armed forces, and appointed and removed public officials. They could veto (stop) any law passed by the legislature and could dissolve (break up) the legislature at any time. And since they were not elected officials, they did not have to worry about being voted out of office for making unpopular decisions.

Parliament, the British legislative body, also created laws for both Britain and the colonies. The colonies sent agents to Britain to try to influence parliamentary decisions, but America did not have representatives in Parliament who could vote on their behalf. For this reason, the colonies were required to obey Parliament's laws,

Britain were allowed to vote. About half of all white American males had voting rights. (Women, servants, and slaves did not have the right to vote in either Britain or America, nor were they allowed to hold public office or to own property.) Americans could elect their own legislators, giving citizens some influence in the making of laws. This system gave many Americans a sense of independence unequaled in any European nation.

The British Parliament is divided into two chambers, the House of Commons and the House of Lords (right).

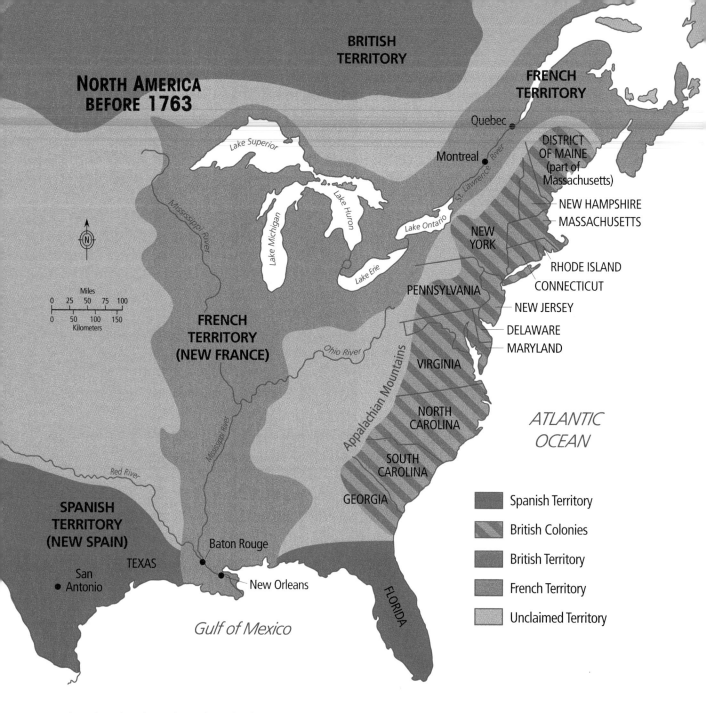

NORTH AMERICA BEFORE 1763

BRITISH TERRITORY

FRENCH TERRITORY

Lake Superior

Quebec

Montreal

DISTRICT OF MAINE (part of Massachusetts)

NEW HAMPSHIRE

MASSACHUSETTS

Lake Michigan

Lake Huron

Lake Ontario

Mississippi River

NEW YORK

RHODE ISLAND

CONNECTICUT

Lake Erie

PENNSYLVANIA

NEW JERSEY

DELAWARE

MARYLAND

Miles
0   25   50   75   100

0   50   100   150
Kilometers

FRENCH TERRITORY (NEW FRANCE)

Ohio River

VIRGINIA

Appalachian Mountains

ATLANTIC OCEAN

NORTH CAROLINA

Mississippi River

SOUTH CAROLINA

Red River

GEORGIA

Spanish Territory

SPANISH TERRITORY (NEW SPAIN)

Baton Rouge

British Colonies

British Territory

TEXAS

San Antonio

New Orleans

French Territory

FLORIDA

Unclaimed Territory

Gulf of Mexico

despite the fact that they had no voice in their creation.

THE FRENCH AND INDIAN WAR

The rich resources and vast territory of North America attracted other European kingdoms. French settlers claimed New France—the land north and west of the British colonies. Spanish settlers claimed much of the land south and west of the French and British colonies, including Florida, calling this area New Spain.

By the mid–1700s, the growing population of the British colonies was forcing many settlers to move westward in search of new land. This westward movement led to clashes with the French. Many Native Americans were also eager to stop British colonists from moving westward and invading their lands. These Indians allied with the French to wage war on the British. The resulting conflict, known as the French and Indian War, lasted nine years (1754–1763). American colonists fought alongside British forces, helping Britain to win the war. The peace treaty signed in 1763 gave Britain all of New France as well as Florida.

King George III

King George III became king of Great Britain upon his grandfather's death in 1760. With his crown, the twenty-two-year-old king inherited a host of challenges. The long war against the French had left the British government with a huge debt. And, by taking control of all of New France, Britain had a huge empire to protect—an empire in which many hostile French and Indians lived.

THE PROCLAMATION OF 1763

To avoid another costly war, George III issued the Proclamation of 1763. This document halted all settlement west of the Appalachian Mountains, reserving these lands for Native Americans. British soldiers were stationed on the frontier to guard against Indian or French invasion and to keep Americans from moving westward. The proclamation was unpopular with many Americans. They viewed it as a violation of their basic right to move and live

The French and Indian War

Fighting between the French and the British spread from North America to Europe, North Africa, and India. The war in Europe was known as the Seven Years' War (1756–1763). Nearly every European nation fought on one side or the other in the conflict. The British defeated the French in several battles in Europe, North Africa, India, and the Caribbean.

Britain's victory had been expensive. Fighting on so many fronts had stretched its resources to the limit. The government found itself on the verge of bankruptcy. At the same time, the country's vast new empire needed protection. And to British leaders, it seemed only fair that the American colonies should have to foot some of the bill for the British army that was protecting them.

Many Americans saw the situation differently. With the French defeated, they questioned why an army was needed in the colonies. To protect the Americans—or to control them? These differing viewpoints became the seeds of revolution. As a French diplomat wrote in 1763, "The colonies will no longer need Britain's protection. She [Britain] will call upon them to contribute toward supporting the burdens they have helped to bring on her, and they will answer by striking off their chains."

where they wanted. In addition, many of the French and Indian War campaigns had been fought on these western lands, which Americans living in these territories had fought for the right to own. The proclamation told them to leave. To these colonists, it appeared as if the British had sided with their enemies.

George III's proclamation was followed by the Revenue Act of 1764. This act, popularly known as the Sugar Act, was designed to help pay for the British soldiers stationed in North America. The law actually lowered the duties (taxes) on certain goods imported from Britain, including molasses, a key ingredient of rum. But the act also called for stricter enforcement of customs laws. Avoiding paying the duties became much more difficult for American merchants. They responded with cries of protest.

THE STAMP ACT AND THE QUARTERING ACT

The following year, Parliament passed two more acts. The Quartering Act was created as another way to get the colonies to pay part of the expense of keeping British soldiers in America. It required the colonies to supply the British troops with living quarters, food, and drink. Although the act was unpopular in America, it did not affect a large percentage of the population.

The Stamp Act taxed printed items, such as newspapers, calendars, legal documents, and playing cards—items used by nearly every American. The Stamp Act required all such documents to be printed on special stamped paper sold in government offices by tax collectors known as Stamp Act agents. Suddenly Parliament was digging in the pockets of not just merchants, but of colonists from all walks of life.

News of the Stamp Act created an explosion of protest from America. Although the tax was relatively small in monetary terms, the principle of the matter greatly upset many colonists. Most Americans weren't against paying their fair share of Britain's expenses. The uproar was caused by Parliament's attempt to tax the colonies without their permission or input. Parliament was passing laws that affected the colonies, but the colonies had no representatives—no votes—in Parliament. Soon cries of "No taxation without representation" were heard throughout America.

Before the Stamp Act went into effect, colonial legislatures met to protest Parliament's actions. In Virginia, a young

A British stamp

Protests against the Stamp Act took many forms. Here, a group of defiant colonists burn stamps in their town square.

legislator named Patrick Henry claimed that Parliament could not tax America without its permission. He persuaded the Virginia legislature to approve a series of statements that denied Parliament's right to tax the colonies. These statements, or resolutions, were printed and sent to the legislatures of the other colonies. They became the basis of violent protest across colonial America.

The American colonists also formed secret organizations to fight the new law. The most powerful of these groups was called the Sons of Liberty. Led by radical Patriots such as Samuel Adams, these groups often used violence, in the form of mob attacks, to get their way.

The Sons of Liberty knew they could do little to stop Parliament from ordering new taxes. But they were determined to stop the British from collecting them. Angry mobs destroyed much of the stamped paper before it could be used. The Sons of Liberty also attacked the tax collectors who sold the stamps, often destroying their homes and businesses. They threatened the collectors with bodily harm—or worse—if they didn't give up their jobs. One by one, the Stamp Tax agents resigned from their posts. Without anyone to sell the stamps, the Stamp Act was useless.

Samuel Adams

Samuel Adams (1722–1803) was born in Quincy, Massachusetts, to a wealthy family. He studied at Harvard University, earning a master's degree in 1743. As a young man, Adams tried his hand as a merchant, but his business failed miserably, and he soon found himself broke. But Adams's true calling was politics and journalism. A short, stocky man who suffered from palsy (uncontrollable shaking), he was not a magnetic speaker. But Adams had a gift for writing, and he used his powerful pen to rally citizens to the cause of liberty. Adams's outspoken and forceful personality also attracted like-minded Americans. He remained a key Patriot leader as the disputes between America and Britain evolved into war.

Tarring & Feathering

Tarring and feathering was a form of punishment that dated back to Medieval Europe (ca. A.D. 500–1500). It combined public humiliation with terrible physical pain. Victims (or offenders, depending on how you looked at it) were stripped; covered in sticky, scalding hot tar; and then covered with feathers. This procedure was carried out by an angry mob, which then paraded the humiliated person around for the entire community to see. As painful as the hot tar was on the skin, removing the tar after it had cooled was even more agonizing. Often large chunks of skin came off with it. In some cases, the wounds led to permanent disfigurement and sometimes death from shock or infection.

In addition, the colonies did not allow British goods into American ports. Nor did they allow American ships to deliver goods to Britain. Punishments for defying this boycott often took the form of beatings, destruction of property, and tarring and feathering. The boycott led to financial hardship for many Americans—but it had an even greater effect on British merchants. Soon British businesspeople were protesting to Parliament. Angry cries against the Stamp Act were soon heard from both sides of the Atlantic.

Up to this point, the thirteen colonies had never worked as one. At the time, Americans did not think of themselves as part of a group of united colonies or states. The colony of North Carolina, for example, had little interest in the affairs of the colony of New York. But the Stamp Act caused such an uproar that the American colonies banded together for the first time to protest it.

Representatives from nine of the thirteen colonies formed the Stamp Act Congress. In October 1765, the congress met in New York City and adopted the Declaration of Rights and Grievances. This document disputed Parliament's right to tax the colonies without their permission.

By the end of 1765, it was clear that the Stamp Act would be impossible to enforce. For several months, Parliament bitterly debated the issue before finally repealing the act on March 18, 1766. But at the same time, it also passed the Declaratory Act, which clearly stated that Parliament had the right to impose laws on the colonies. George III and the anti-American members of Parliament were not about to let the

British customs commissioners, backed up by troops, had the right to search colonists' homes and seize goods they suspected had been smuggled.

colonists think they had won the battle. But for the time being, the American boycott on British goods was lifted.

MORE REASONS TO UNITE

In June 1767, Parliament passed a new series of laws called the Townshend Acts, which placed a duty on British imports of glass, lead, paint, tea, and paper. Parliament knew that collecting the taxes and enforcing the Townshend Acts would be difficult. So they set up a customs agency and hired Royal Customs Commissioners to collect the taxes. Parliament gave the commissioners much more power than the Stamp Act

agents had, including the right to search private warehouses and homes for smuggled goods—goods that had entered the colonies without payment of the customs duties. They were also allowed to seize any smuggled goods. And they had the British army and navy to back them up. Once again, American protesters ordered a boycott on British goods.

At this time, a Pennsylvanian named John Dickinson wrote a series of letters called *Letters from a Farmer in Pennsylvania to the Inhabitants of the British Colonies*. Published in newspapers, his letters were addressed, "My Dear Countrymen," and were signed, "A Farmer." (In reality, Dickinson was a lawyer and diplomat.) In simple, clear language, Dickinson explained why Britain's policies violated the colonists' rights. Eventually collected into a pamphlet, the letters were instrumental in shaping colonial opinion.

Other events added to the hostility between the British and the Patriots, as the Americans who openly opposed British policies were called. In 1768 John Hancock, a wealthy merchant and Patriot leader of Boston, Massachussets, became a target of the British customs commissioners. The commissioners knew that Hancock was smuggling goods. They wanted to make an example of him to show the colonists that the British government was in charge. They seized one of Hancock's ships and accused him of violating regulations. Angry Bostonians swarmed the harbor and docks in protest. News reached London that Boston was in a state of revolt. In response, George III sent British troops to Boston to control future Patriot uprisings. They arrived in late 1768.

Many Bostonians deeply resented the redcoats, as the red-uniformed soldiers were called. To the Americans, the soldiers represented an unjust king and Parliament. The redcoats and the citizens often exchanged insults, many of which led to fistfights. Some sort of confrontation seemed inevitable.

British authorities considered John Hancock (*above*) to be one of America's most dangerous revolutionaries.

BLOOD IN
2 THE STREETS

The situation finally exploded on the evening of March 5, 1770. The trouble started when a Bostonian shouted an insult at a British soldier. The soldier responded by whacking the American on the head. Word of the incident spread throughout town.

The British soldier soon found himself surrounded by "an irresponsible mob of some 60 rioters." Pelted by sticks, stones, and snowballs, he called for help. Seven soldiers and an officer came to his aid. The angry mob closed in on the frightened redcoats. Fearing for their lives, the soldiers fired into the crowd. Three colonists died at the scene. Two more died later from

their wounds. Samuel Adams and other Patriot leaders demanded that the soldiers be hung (a common form of execution in colonial America) in the city square. Thomas Hutchinson, the British-appointed lieutenant governor of Massachusetts, immediately declared that the soldiers would be put on trial. He also moved the British troops to an island in Boston Harbor to prevent further violence.

The Sons of Liberty used the event for propaganda, to further stir up anger against the British. A Bostonian named Paul Revere made an engraving of the scene. His famous—and inaccurate—

Boston Massacre

The British soldiers involved in the Boston Massacre were tried for murder in the fall of 1770. Two American lawyers, John Adams *(right)* and Josiah Quincy, accepted the unpopular task of defending the soldiers in court. Although Adams was a Patriot (and a cousin of Samuel Adams), he also believed that all people in a free country deserve a fair trial. To the surprise of many, the jury found the British officer and five of the British soldiers innocent. The two others were convicted of manslaughter but were later released from jail after being dismissed from the army.

portrayal showed smiling British troops firing on surprised civilians. Samuel Adams named the event the Boston Massacre, describing it as "a plot to massacre the inhabitants of Boston."

By April 12, 1770, Parliament had voted to repeal most of the Townshend Acts. But, in another move to demonstrate their authority over the Americans, they chose to leave one tax in place—the tax on tea.

For the next few years, few conflicts arose between the Americans and the British. The boycott against British goods was once again abandoned. But Patriot leaders such as Samuel Adams continued to speak out against British rule. In 1772 he and other Sons of Liberty began forming committees of correspondence, which shared information about protest activities.

This peaceful situation changed in the spring of 1773, when Parliament passed the Tea Act. Up to this time, British tea had been more expensive than tea smuggled from other countries. The new law made British tea cheaper—and the British

Paul Revere's engraving is an inaccurate depiction of the Boston Massacre. In fact, the British troops were cornered by a mob that vastly outnumbered them.

In this and many other images, the Boston Tea Party is shown as a riotous celebration. In fact, the dumping of the tea was a quick, orderly, and relatively quiet affair.

government would still be able to collect a tax from it. But a tax was a tax, no matter how Parliament presented it. And to many Patriots, such a tax was still a violation of their liberty.

In Boston, Samuel Adams and the Sons of Liberty set out to stop the Tea Act. They called for a boycott against British tea. Then Adams and the Patriots took their protest one step further.

BOSTON TEA PARTY

On November 28, 1773, three ships carrying cargoes of British tea arrived in Boston. The Patriots demanded that the tea be sent back to Britain. Governor Hutchinson refused to give in to their demands.

EYEWITNESS QUOTE:
BOSTON TEA PARTY

"Perfect regularity prevailed during the whole transaction. . . . entire silence prevailed—no clamor, no talking. Nothing was meddled with but the teas on board. After having emptied the hold, the deck was swept clean, and everything put in its proper place. An officer on board was requested to come up from the cabin and see that no damage was done except to the tea."

—Robert Sessions,
Boston Patriot

On December 16, 1773, about fifty Sons of Liberty dressed up as Mohawk Indians and swarmed onto the harbor docks. Crowds of spectators lined up to watch as the Patriots boarded the ships. With tidy efficiency, they broke open the chests of tea with axes and dumped the tea into the harbor. The next morning, Boston Harbor was a sea of sludge. The Sons of Liberty had destroyed thousands of dollars worth of tea. When word of the Boston Tea Party reached Britain, George III and Parliament were furious. They quickly passed a series of laws, known in Britain as the Coercive Acts, designed to punish Boston.

Governor Hutchinson

One of the Coercive Acts ordered Boston Harbor closed until Bostonians paid for the tea they had destroyed. Starting on June 1, 1774, British warships made sure nothing—no vessels of any kind, not a stick of lumber, not a bale of hay—was allowed into or out of the port. All fishers, merchants, and other Bostonians who depended on the port were out of business. British troops were ordered back into the city.

Parliament had sent a loud and clear message to the colonies—respect and follow the laws of Britain or suffer the consequences. But these acts, called the Intolerable Acts in America, only served to further unite the colonies against Britain. The Patriots called for representatives from the colonies to meet in Philadelphia, Pennsylvania, at the First Continental Congress. The purpose of this meeting was to decide on a response to the Intolerable Acts.

On September 5, 1774, fifty-six men representing twelve of the thirteen colonies met in Philadelphia. (Only the colony of Georgia did not send representatives.) The group included Samuel and John Adams, George Washington, Patrick Henry, and John Hancock.

None of the delegates called for independence. Instead, they recorded their complaints against Britain and declared their rights as colonists. Once again, a boycott on British goods was declared. The congress also ordered the colonies to form militias—citizen armies—to defend themselves. Each colonial town and city had a local militia, composed of male volunteers. A select group of these men were known as minutemen, as they pledged to be ready to fight at a minute's notice. Throughout America, Patriots were raid-

Following the Boston Tea Party, British warships closed Boston Harbor. The closing brought severe economic hardship to the city and rallied other colonies to the Patriot cause.

ing British arsenals (places to store weapons) and stealing guns and gunpowder. The Americans weren't calling for war, but they were preparing for it, just in case.

READY FOR A FIGHT

George III and Parliament refused to even consider the Continental Congress's complaints. They had no intention of negotiating with the unruly Americans. On February 2, 1775, the king declared Massachusetts to be in rebellion. This was more or less a declaration of war against the colony. A peaceful solution to the conflict seemed impossible.

In early April, Governor-General Thomas Gage—the commander in chief of the British military in North America who had replaced Hutchinson as the royal governor of Massachusetts—received secret orders from Britain. He was to capture Samuel Adams and John Hancock and to seize the Massachusetts Patriots' stolen

A group of Patriots seizes a wagon carrying British weapons and ammunition.

stockpiles of ammunition. But Patriot leaders caught wind of the plan. Paul Revere and another Bostonian, William Dawes, were assigned the job of sounding the alarm should British troops go on the march.

On the night of April 18, 1775, seven hundred British soldiers moved out of Boston. Their mission was to capture the rebel leaders Adams and Hancock in Lexington, a town about ten miles northwest of Boston. They were then to seize the military supplies stored in Concord, about five miles farther down the road.

Patriot spies quickly sent word to Revere and Dawes. The two men—the midnight riders, as they later came to be known—set off to alert the countryside. The warning system worked. By 3:00 A.M., the alarm had been spread from Boston to

The Continental Association

The First Continental Congress adopted a document known as the Continental Association. It called upon cities, towns, and counties to form Committees of Inspection to enforce the boycott on British trade. These committees wielded great power. Citizens who were caught violating the boycott could be condemned as enemies of American liberty. Such a condemnation often meant exclusion from the community, if not harassment or even bodily harm. In many cases, these committees went on to become the local branches of the Continental Congress.

Tewksbury, twenty-five miles north, and to Concord, sixteen miles west. Minutemen picked up their muskets (rifles) and set out to face the British. They were ready for a fight.

BATTLES OF LEXINGTON AND CONCORD

By dawn on April 19, 1775, a group of minutemen had gathered at the center of town in Lexington. Led by Captain John Parker, the group included a sixty-three year old, a seventy-four year old, eight fathers and their sons, a slave, and twelve teenagers—hardly a match for the seven hundred redcoats headed their way.

Riding ahead of the main British force, four British officers on horseback confronted Parker's minutemen. Behind them, the redcoats moved in. One British officer shouted, "Lay down your arms!" Badly outnumbered, Captain Parker ordered his men to go home. The minutemen began to leave. But they did not lay down their weapons.

Exactly what happened next is still a mystery. A shot was fired. British witnesses say it was an American who fired this shot. Americans claim one of the British officers fired first. Whatever the case, the British soldiers responded with a hail of musket balls. The Lexington minutemen ran for cover and began firing back at the British. Moments later, the skirmish was over. Eight Americans lay dead. Ten were wounded. Only one British soldier was hurt.

Midnight Riders

As the British troops moved out of Boston, William Dawes raced ahead of them. He shouted to local militias along the way, "The British are coming, sound the alarm!" At the same time, Paul Revere mounted Brown Beauty, one of the fastest horses in New England. Galloping through the countryside at breakneck speed (right), Revere reached Lexington in time to warn Hancock and Adams. He also alerted the militia and other messengers along the way. These messengers fanned out across the countryside, spreading news of the British march.

At Lexington, Dawes and Revere were joined by a third rider, Dr. Samuel Prescott, for the journey to Concord. But the three Patriots were captured by a British patrol. They all managed to escape, but Revere was caught again. Dawes fled back to Lexington, while Prescott rode on to Concord to sound the alarm. The midnight riders, as they came to be known, succeeded in warning the Patriots in Lexington and Concord of the British army's movements. The alert gave the Patriots time to hide their illegal weapons and ammunition.

The minor battle that erupted in the Lexington town square on April 19, 1775, was the beginning of a bloody day for the British troops and their Patriot counterparts.

After Lexington, the British troops continued their march to Concord. The Concord militia, knowing they faced a British force that outnumbered them, had already moved out of town. There they waited for more minutemen to arrive. At Concord, the British searched homes and storerooms but found few guns and little ammunition. The townspeople had been up most of the night hiding their illegal supplies. What the British did find, they set ablaze in a bonfire in the center of town.

Seeing smoke rising from their town, the Concord militia decided to attack. A short, fierce battle erupted. The Americans fell back and the British gathered for a return to Boston.

Meanwhile, word of the British attack at Lexington had spread throughout the area. Hundreds of militiamen poured in from the countryside. As the redcoats marched out of Concord, they were attacked by swarms of Americans. Instead of confronting the British head on, the Patriot fighters used the hit-and-run fighting techniques they had learned in the French and Indian War.

> **EYEWITNESS QUOTE:**
> **BATTLE OF CONCORD**
>
> "We were fired on from all sides . . . hills, woods, stone walls, etc., . . . were all lined with people who kept incessant fire upon us, . . . [T]hey were so concealed there was hardly any seeing them. In this way, we marched . . . miles, their numbers increasing from all parts, while ours was reducing by deaths, wounds, and fatigue."
>
> **—a British lieutenant**

THE BRITISH POINT OF VIEW

British policy toward America was dictated by George III, his ministers, and Parliament. The king and his prime minister, Lord North, arranged bribes to make sure the British legislature had a majority that sided with the king. This power allowed King George and his ministers to pursue the war, despite the fact that the public did not support it.

Lord North

Beginning with the events surrounding the Stamp Act in 1765, George III was determined to punish the colonies for their rebellious behavior. In 1774 the king wrote, "I am not sorry to see that...blows must decide whether they [the colonies] are to be subject to this country or independent." The king's unwillingness even to listen to colonial grievances made a negotiated settlement between the two sides impossible.

Some members of Parliament did speak out against Britain's approach to the colonies. William Pitt, a former prime minister, harshly criticized the policies that led to the conflict with America. Edmund Burke and Charles James Fox were two other prominent politicians who openly opposed the war. But these men were in the minority in Parliament. Their protests were largely ignored.

A number of high-ranking officers in the British army and navy refused to serve in America. Said the earl of Effingham, a high-ranking army officer, "I cannot, without reproach [blame] from my conscience, consent to bear arms against my fellow subjects in America in what . . . is not a clear cause."

The common British citizen had little sympathy for the colonists or their complaints. They were already burdened with taxation. And since only a small percentage of the British population was allowed to vote, Parliament did not truly represent their interests either. To most British people, the Americans' protests were obnoxious.

The majority of British citizens, rich and poor, considered the colonists castoffs from British society—backwoods country bumpkins, criminals, the lowest of the low. But the war against America was never popular among the masses in Britain. War meant more and higher taxes. It meant the loss of loved ones fighting overseas. But perhaps the war's greatest impact was in the loss of the money-making trade between Britain and America. The war brought economic hardship to many British citizens. Protests from merchants and manufacturers grew louder as the war went on.

Patriot soldiers *(foreground)* fired musket balls at British troops as the British retreated from Lexington to Boston.

The British march back to Boston covered sixteen miles. At times it appeared that the redcoats might be completely wiped out by the marauding Americans. By the time the British reached safety, night had fallen. Seventy-three redcoats had been killed. Two hundred were wounded or missing. About forty Americans had been killed in the battle. The quarrel between Britain and America had exploded into a deadly conflict.

After the Battles of Lexington and Concord, Massachusetts Patriots feared the British army would seek revenge for its humiliating defeat. The Patriots sent out a call to other colonies for reinforcements. Thousands of militiamen from Connecticut, Rhode Island, New Hampshire, and Massachusetts answered, gathering a force of about fifteen thousand. This large group began building fortifications around Boston to blockade, or trap, the British army inside the city. Although few realized it at the time, the events of Lexington and Concord marked the beginning of a long and costly war.

3 WAR FOR AMERICA

With Governor-General Thomas Gage's army bottled up in Boston, Patriot leaders feared that the British would invade Massachusetts from bases in the colony of New York and in Canada. These strongholds included Fort Ticonderoga, which lay at the southern end of Lake Champlain in western New York. Patriot leaders knew the fort was lightly guarded and would be an easy target for an American attack.

On May 10, 1775, two groups of Patriot militia, under the joint command of Colonel Benedict Arnold and Ethan Allen, descended on Fort Ticonderoga. The small unit of British defenders was completely surprised, and the Patriots took the fort without any serious injuries on either side. The victory won the Patriots more than eighty artillery pieces (cannons) and thousands of cannonballs, as well as control of an important base. American forces then moved northward to capture a second British fort at Crown Point, New York.

SECOND CONTINENTAL CONGRESS
On that same day, unaware of Arnold and Allen's adventures in New York, the Continental Congress met for a second time.

In response to the bloody events at Lexington and Concord, the delegates voted to turn the fifteen thousand militiamen camped outside of Boston into a Continental Army. This army would unite the many different colonial militias into one single command. George Washington of Virginia was selected as the army's commander in chief.

BATTLE AT BREED'S HILL (BUNKER HILL)

In late May 1775, more British troops landed in Boston. Arriving with them were three generals, William Howe, Henry Clinton, and John Burgoyne. George III had lost confidence in General Gage and had sent the three generals to America to crush the colonial rebellion once and for all.

But first, the British forces would have to break out of Boston. To do this, the generals developed a plan to seize the Charlestown Peninsula, a high ground overlooking Boston and its harbor. Taking control of the area would protect the British force inside of Boston from an American attack from that direction. Holding the heights would also provide the British with a position from which to launch an attack to drive the American troops away from Boston.

An invasion of the Charlestown Peninsula was set for mid-June. But Patriot spies caught wind of the plan. The militiamen in the area moved quickly to outmaneuver the British. On the night of June 16, 1775, twelve hundred Americans moved onto the peninsula. Working through the night, the men furiously dug out trenches and built dirt walls on Breed's Hill in the center of the peninsula. Early the next morning, the British awoke to find a Patriot

Benedict Arnold

Benedict Arnold (1741–1801) was born in Norwich, Connecticut. As a young man, he worked as an apprentice in his cousins's apothecary (pharmacy) business. Arnold established his own apothecary in New Haven, Connecticut, where he became a well known and respected member of the community. Expanding his business, Arnold became a successful merchant, transporting goods to and from the West Indies. The Stamp Act and the other British customs laws that followed had a direct effect on Arnold's business. Outspoken and combative, he quickly became a Patriot leader in protests against British policies. At the time the Battles of Lexington and Concord broke out, Arnold was serving as a captain in the New Hampshire militia. Upon hearing the news of the fighting, Arnold immediately offered his services to the Patriot cause.

As British cannonballs whizzed past, Patriot commander William Prescott stood on the wall of the Bunker Hill fort to steady his frightened men.

fort in the place they had planned to occupy. If the British were going to take the peninsula, they would have to fight for it.

British warships began firing on the American fort. Cannonballs exploded around the militiamen. Soon, hundreds of British troops had landed. Led by General Howe, the redcoats gathered in tight formations and began a slow, steady march up the hill toward the Patriots.

Behind the fort's walls, the Americans aimed their muskets at the advancing redcoats. The Patriots had only a small amount of ammunition. Every shot counted. William Prescott, their commander, had ordered them to hold their fire "until you can see the whites of their eyes."

When the redcoats were within fifty yards, the fort erupted in a blaze of musket fire and smoke. Many of the first line of British troops were cut down by militia gunfire. The lines behind them continued to march forward, stepping over their fallen comrades.

The Americans held off two British attacks before running out of ammunition. When a third wave of redcoats stormed the fort, the militiamen tried to defend themselves by using their muskets as clubs. But a swinging rifle was no match for British bayonets (the blades attached to the end of the soldiers' muskets). The Patriots were quickly overwhelmed and forced to retreat.

As the American militiamen fled, British commanders argued over whether or not to pursue them. General Clinton urged General Howe to continue the attack, seeing an opportunity to destroy the American forces right then and there. Howe, a cautious soldier, rejected this idea.

The British had taken command of the hill and its fort—but at a terrible cost. More than two hundred British soldiers had been killed. Nearly nine hundred had been wounded. American losses were estimated to be 140 men killed, 301 wounded.

EYEWITNESS QUOTE:
BUNKER HILL

"As fast as the front man was shot down, the next stepped forward into his place. . . . It was surprising how they would step over their dead bodies, as though they had been logs of wood."

—a Patriot militiaman

The Battle of Bunker Hill or Breed's Hill?

The battle that took place on Breed's Hill has come down through history as the Battle of Bunker Hill. When Patriot military leaders first chose to build a fort on the Charlestown Peninsula, they could not decide which hill to build it on. Bunker Hill was the higher of the two hills but was farther away from Boston—too far away for Patriot cannons to reach British positions. Breed's Hill, located at the center of the peninsula, was not as steep but was closer to Boston. Patriot leaders chose Breed's Hill as the site for the fort. At the time, the two hills were often considered to be one single, connected hill—Bunker Hill. This is why the battle came to be known as Bunker Hill.

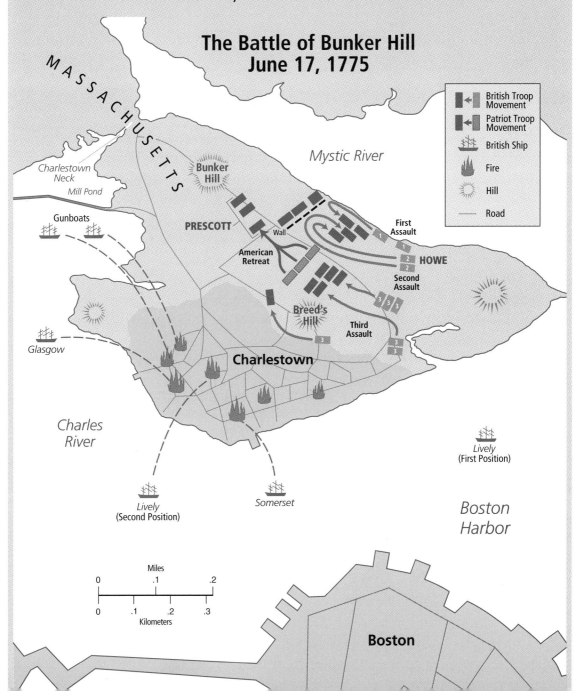

The Battle of Bunker Hill
June 17, 1775

MASSACHUSETTS

Mystic River

Legend:
- British Troop Movement
- Patriot Troop Movement
- British Ship
- Fire
- Hill
- Road

Charlestown Neck

Mill Pond

Bunker Hill

Gunboats

PRESCOTT

Wall

First Assault

American Retreat

HOWE

Second Assault

Breed's Hill

Third Assault

Glasgow

Charlestown

Charles River

Lively (Second Position)

Somerset

Lively (First Position)

Boston Harbor

Miles
0 .1 .2

0 .1 .2 .3
Kilometers

Boston

Patriot muskets cut down the first waves of British troops that tried to storm Breed's Hill. But after the Patriots ran out of ammunition, the British, armed with bayonets, forced the Americans to flee.

At first, the Americans viewed the battle as a horrible defeat. But in the following weeks, the militiamen realized that they had won a victory of sorts. They had learned that the British army was not unbeatable. And they had shown the British that American troops could not be taken lightly. "I wish we could sell them another hill at the same price," said one American general.

WASHINGTON MEETS HIS ARMY

Two weeks after Bunker Hill, George Washington arrived to take command of the new Continental Army. He was shocked by the state of the troops. As citizen soldiers, the militiamen had little respect for Washington and his officers. They resisted discipline and knew little, if anything, about military procedures. Since the soldiers were volunteers, they had only agreed to serve until the end of the year.

To make matters worse, Washington's ragtag army was desperately short on ammunition, weapons, clothing, guns, medical supplies, and food—not to mention money to pay the soldiers. The Continental Congress had agreed to pay for the army. But because the congress could not tax citizens, it had no way to collect money for supplies and pay. Washington could only ask congress, which could ask the colonial governments, which could ask the colonists for money. As Washington would soon learn, this was not an efficient way to run a war.

DECLARATION OF WAR

When reports of the Battle of Bunker Hill reached Britain, George III and Parliament were shocked by the losses. Said one member of Parliament, "Eight more such 'victories' and we shall have no one left to report them!" George III issued the Proclamation of Rebellion on August 23, 1775. Instead of just declaring war against Massachusetts, as they had done in February, George III and Parliament declared all of the colonies to be in rebellion. The king replaced General Gage with General Howe as commander in chief of British forces. No battles took place in Boston for the rest of the year.

The colonies covered a huge territory. They had no nerve center, such as a national capital, that the British could conquer and thus cripple the American war effort. Instead, the British and Americans attempted to seize key cities and locations.

Still worried about a British invasion from the north, the Patriots wanted to control the route from British-held Canada to Massachusetts. To do this, General Washington sent a force to capture the cities of Montreal and Quebec in Canada in late 1775.

George Washington

George Washington (1732–1799) was born in Virginia, the son of a wealthy planter. He had little formal education, but by age sixteen, he was working as a surveyor, mapping the wilderness of western Virginia. Washington's intelligence, quiet dignity, and commanding presence—he stood six feet two inches tall—made him an excellent candidate for military and political leadership. In 1752 he was given a commission as a major in the Virginia militia, despite having no military training or experience. Washington went on to fight in several key battles in the French and Indian War. By age twenty-six, he was the most famous American-born soldier in the colonies.

Washington's prestige earned him a seat in the Virginia legislature in 1758, where he served for fifteen years. Elected as a delegate to the First Continental Congress in 1774, he worked to pass a boycott on British goods to protest British policies.

At the Second Continental Congress in June 1775, Washington wore his military uniform from the French and Indian War to show his support for the Patriot cause. His experience, fame, and confidence made him an obvious choice for commander in chief of the Continental Army. The Congress unanimously elected him to the post. Washington was honored, but he said, "I do not think my self equal to the command." He refused to be paid for his service.

MINORITIES IN THE AMERICAN REVOLUTION

"Liberty" was the great rallying cry of the American Revolution. But at the time, the freedom and rights claimed by the colonies did not apply to African American slaves, Native Americans, or white women. When war broke out, many nonwhite people in America found themselves in the middle of the conflict.

Native Americans At the start of the war, the British government lured many tribes into the conflict with clothes, guns, ammunition, and other goods. In addition, many Indians agreed to fight because they wanted to stop Americans from moving onto their lands. Historians estimate that about thirteen thousand Native Americans fought for the British during the war, including the two largest Indian confederations, the Iroquois and the Cherokee. (A much smaller number of Indians, including the Oneida, sided with the Americans.)

These British-supported warriors had some success against small white settlements on the frontier. But such attacks usually provoked overwhelming responses from American forces. Patriots raided and destroyed Indian villages, burning crops and slaughtering livestock. When the British abandoned the war, the Indians who had fought for them were treated harshly by Americans. According to the victorious Americans, these native peoples had chosen the wrong side and deserved such treatment.

African Americans In 1776, 99 percent of African Americans were slaves. Both British and Patriot leaders promised freedom to some of these blacks in return for service in their respective armies. Thousands served on both sides. Historians estimate that African American soldiers made up 15 percent of the Continental Army by 1779. By 1782 twenty thousand South Carolina slaves alone had served with the British.

A slave auction advertisement

Some African American soldiers did earn their freedom. But many of the promises made by the British and the Americans were never fulfilled. Many blacks who had served with the British were sent back to their masters when the war ended. American blacks who were captured by the British often suffered a horrible fate. Many were sold to sugar plantations in the West Indies, where they died from overwork. But African Americans' participation in the Patriot struggle did help change some whites' opinions about slavery. By the end of the war, Vermont, Massachusetts, and New Hampshire had abolished slavery. And Pennsylvania, Rhode Island, and Connecticut voted to free slaves in these states over a period of years.

WOMEN IN THE AMERICAN REVOLUTION

Abigail Adams was just one of many women eager to play a larger role in America at the time of the revolution. She hoped that a new code of laws would be created in which women were granted more rights and opportunities. Before the war, a woman's place was in the home. Women could not vote, hold public office, or own property. But the onset of the war gave some women the opportunity to show their value to society in a public way. Esther DeBerdt Reed, founder of the Ladies Association of Philadelphia, urged women of the era to "aspire to render themselves more really useful" and to "emulate the deeds of great ancient heroines."

Some women contributed to the cause by risking their lives on the field of battle. Deborah Sampson disguised herself as a man and enlisted in the Continental Army in 1782. Using the name Robert Shurtleff, she was stationed at the fortress at West Point, New York, and saw action on more than one occasion. After her identity was discovered, Sampson was granted a pension (payment for service) by the government.

Deborah Sampson

Betty Zane risked her life to supply surrounded troops with gunpowder in one of the last battles of the revolution. At the siege of Fort Henry, the sixteen-year-old delivered the powder under a hail of enemy fire. She was praised as the hero of the fight.

Other women chose less dangerous ways to aid the Patriot cause. Many contributed from the home front by starting volunteer societies, making musket balls and uniforms, and managing stores and farms while their husbands were away. Elizabeth Adkins remarked that after her husband was drafted, she "had to plough and hoe his corn to raise bread for the children." In the middle of the war, Patriot leader Dr. Benjamin Rush wrote, "The women of America have at last become principals in the glorious American controversy."

By the time the war had ended, many women had made significant contributions. But Abigail Adams's dream of laws that would provide women with new freedoms did not become reality. Employment opportunities were still limited for women, and men remained masters of both the home and society. Many more generations of struggle lay ahead before women won the basic rights modern Americans enjoy.

American soldiers invaded Quebec in the teeth of a raging blizzard. The attack was a disaster. The American commander was killed, Benedict Arnold was wounded, and three hundred American soldiers were taken prisoner.

The Americans, led by Benedict Arnold and others, conquered Montreal. But the invasion of Quebec, launched during a howling blizzard, failed. Canada's key city remained in British hands, and the threat of a northern invasion remained.

Meanwhile, Americans loyal to George III were attempting to gain control of the southern colonies. The British believed that most southern colonists remained loyal to Britain. They hoped to recruit these Loyalists, as they came to be called, to fight against Patriots in the south.

But instead of gaining followers, Lord Dunmore, the royal governor of Virginia, enraged many potential Loyalists. He urged slaves belonging to Patriots to escape from their masters and join the British cause. This action outraged many southern colonists, who feared the loss of people they considered their private property. As a result, many potential Loyalists turned against the British.

In late 1775 and early 1776, Loyalist and British forces suffered a series of defeats in Virginia, North Carolina, South Carolina, and Georgia. By the spring of 1776, Patriots controlled the governments of all of these southern colonies.

FAST FACT

THE FIRST SOUTHERN BATTLES

In Virginia, Patriots and Loyalists clashed at Great Bridge, near Norfolk, in November 1775. Months later, on February 27, 1776, North Carolinian Patriots and Loyalists fought at Moore's Creek Bridge, near Wilmington. Loyalists were soundly defeated in both battles.

Patriot, Loyalist, or Neutral?

Patriots were colonists who openly and actively opposed British policies. Led by men such as Samuel Adams and John Hancock, they were the first to protest the unpopular Parliamentary laws of the 1760s. Eventually, Patriots took up arms against British troops and led America into war. Historians estimate that about one-third of American colonists were Patriots.

Loyalists were American colonists who remained loyal to George III and Britain. Although many disagreed with Britain's taxation policies, they continued to support the mother country. When war broke out, many Loyalists fought alongside the British. Approximately one-third of American colonists remained loyal to the Britain.

A Loyalist being "drummed out of town"

The remaining one-third of the American population stayed neutral during the war—they refused to take sides. However, many Americans changed their allegiances during the course of the conflict.

Despite the spreading violence, most Americans were not ready to break ties with Britain. They still considered themselves loyal British subjects whom George III and Parliament had treated unfairly.

Most Americans hoped that George III would be reasonable and call for an end to the conflict. But in December 1775, Parliament made another warlike gesture by passing the Prohibitory Act, which ordered the British Royal Navy to seize American ships.

Then, in January 1776, a 47-page pamphlet, titled *Common Sense*, boldly attacked

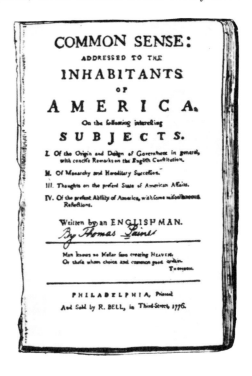

Common Sense remains one of the best-selling books in American history.

Thomas Paine

The anonymous author of *Common Sense* was Thomas Paine (1737–1809). He was born and raised in Britain. As a young man, he tried several occupations, including sailor, schoolteacher, tobacconist, and grocer, failing at all of them. In 1774 Paine moved to America. There he found his true calling as a journalist for the *Pennsylvania Magazine* in Philadelphia. Paine's straightforward articles could be read and understood by common people as well as intellectuals. In addition to *Common Sense*, Paine also published *The American Crisis*, in late 1776. Written during the darkest days of the war, it began, "These are the times that try men's souls. . . ." The words provided encouragement to Patriots at a time when the war seemed all but lost.

George III and Parliament. Its anonymous author defended the Patriots' actions and their right to declare independence from Britain if the king continued his unfair policies.

The pamphlet's fiery words took America by storm. By the spring of 1776, more than one hundred thousand copies of *Common Sense* had been printed and distributed throughout the colonies. For the first time, thousands of colonists had the chance to read the Patriot point of view, in simple, logical words. *Common Sense* triggered a revolution in the hearts and minds of many Americans. The concept of independence from Britain became a far less radical idea.

A NATION
4 IS BORN

While *Common Sense* was spreading throughout the colonies, Washington was working on a plan to take back Boston from the British. But he needed heavy weapons, such as cannons and other artillery. The Patriots had captured a number of such weapons the year before at Fort Ticonderoga. But the weapons were more than three hundred miles away from where Washington needed them.

Washington gave a plucky young colonel named Henry Knox the difficult task of transporting the weaponry to the Continental Army. Working in the dead of winter, Knox and his men used forty-two sleds pulled by 160 oxen to transport the sixty tons of weapons and ammunition over the icy, rugged, muddy landscape.

On the night of March 2, 1776, the Americans set up the cannons and began bombarding Boston. But this attack was only a diversion. Two nights later, Washington sent a huge force of Continental soldiers to Dorchester Heights, a hill on the peninsula south of Boston. This position overlooked the city. His men worked through the night, building a massive network of fortifications. As at Bunker Hill, the British awoke the following morning to a shocking sight—a massive network of American forts and dozens of cannons pointed at them.

Washington's bold plan called for a massive bombardment and invasion of the

Henry Knox *(above)*, a former bookseller, was one of Washington's most trusted officers.

city. By attacking from several different directions, he hoped to trap the British inside of Boston and, with one swift stroke, win the war for the Patriots.

But, by this time, the British had already begun to move out of the city. Still, Washington hoped to invade and capture as much of the British force as possible before they could escape. But a violent thunderstorm rolled in on the night of March 5. Washington was forced to call off the attack. By March 17, the British had loaded up their ships and had abandoned Boston.

The Continental Army celebrated its victory. But Washington was disappointed.

Richard Henry Lee *(right)* of Virginia was one of the Continental Congress's most vocal supporters of independence.

He had hoped to destroy the British army. He knew General Howe would return to fight again. And he was sure where the British general would turn up: New York, a major center of American trade.

THE DECLARATION OF INDEPENDENCE

As the summer of 1776 approached, news came that George III had hired eighteen thousand mercenaries (paid professional soldiers) from parts of southern Germany. These men were being sent to help the British wage war on the Americans. Many Americans finally understood that the king was not working toward a peaceful settlement to the dispute. The call for independence grew ever louder.

On June 7, 1776, Richard Henry Lee, a Virginia delegate to the Continental Congress in Philadelphia, introduced a resolution. It stated, "That these United Colonies are, and of right ought to be, free and independent States. . . . and that all political connection between them and the

Hessians

The German mercenaries *(right)* who fought in the American Revolution were commonly known as Hessians. This is because many of them came from the German states of Hesse-Cassel and Hesse-Hanau. (At the time, the area that later became Germany was divided into some three hundred states.) Loaning out men to fight was very profitable for the rulers of these states. In total, about thirty thousand German officers and soldiers fought for the British. Although a large number of Germans volunteered for service, many men were simply taken from their homes and forced to serve against their will. Most German troops fought well and bravely throughout the war. Some seven thousand died in battle or from disease or illness. Approximately another five thousand deserted from the army, choosing to make America their new home.

State of Great Britain is, and ought to be totally dissolved. . . . "

Lee's resolution gave voice to what more Americans were thinking. The delegates appointed a committee to write a formal declaration that would expand Lee's statement.

A lawyer from Virginia, Thomas Jefferson, was assigned to write the declaration. Working for seventeen days and nights, Jefferson crafted the Declaration of Independence. With a few changes from the committee and members of the congress, Jefferson's draft was presented to the Continental Congress on June 28, 1776. The next step was to debate the declaration.

By the time debate began on July 1, most of the delegates had already agreed to independence. The others were merely waiting for approval from their home colonies. On July 2, 1776, all thirteen colonies voted for independence, and a new nation—the United States of America—was born.

Thomas Jefferson *(left)* considered the Declaration of Independence "an expression of the American mind."

John Adams, one of the delegates who had pushed hardest for independence, wrote to his wife, Abigail, that July 2 "ought to be celebrated, as the day of deliverance [freedom]. . . . It ought to be . . . [celebrated] with pomp and parade, with shows, games, sports, guns, bells, bonfires, and . . . [fireworks], from one end of this continent to the other, from this time forward, evermore." Such celebrations do take place every year in the United States. But instead they take place on July 4, the day the declaration was officially adopted by the congress. The joyous ringing of the Liberty Bell in Philadelphia announced the news.

In the days that followed, word spread throughout the colonies. While Loyalists mourned, Patriots celebrated. But plans and documents meant little when the British army and navy still lurked off American shores. To declare independence was one matter. To make independence a reality, the new United States would have to fight—and defeat—the world's greatest military power.

The Declaration of Independence

The Declaration of Independence has four main sections. The following are passages from each:

The Preamble (introductory statement): When in the Course of human events, it becomes necessary for one people to dissolve the political bands which have connected them with another. . . . [a] decent respect to the opinions of mankind requires that they should declare the causes which impel [drive] them to the separation.

A Declaration of Rights: We hold these truths to be self-evident, that all men are created equal, that they are endowed by their Creator with certain unalienable [incapable of being surrendered] Rights, that among these are Life, Liberty, and the pursuit of Happiness.

A Bill of Indictment (a list of offenses committed by George III against the colonies): Such has been the patient sufferance of these Colonies; and such is now the necessity which constrains [forces] them to alter their former Systems of Government.

A Statement of Independence: We, therefore, the Representatives of the united States of America . . . solemnly publish and declare, That these United Colonies are, and of Right ought to be Free and Independent States.

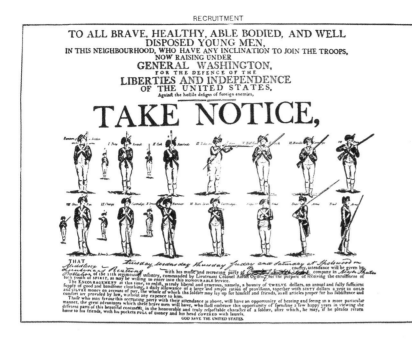

RECRUITMENT

TO ALL BRAVE, HEALTHY, ABLE BODIED, AND WELL DISPOSED YOUNG MEN, IN THIS NEIGHBOURHOOD, WHO HAVE ANY INCLINATION TO JOIN THE TROOPS, NOW RAISING UNDER GENERAL WASHINGTON, FOR THE DEFENCE OF THE LIBERTIES AND INDEPENDENCE OF THE UNITED STATES.

TAKE NOTICE,

This poster calls on all able-bodied Patriot men to enlist. It promises recruits a "bounty of twelve dollars, an annual and fully sufficient supply of good and handsome cloathing, a daily allowance of a large and ample ration of provisions [food], together with sixty dollars a year in gold and silver money." The Continental Congress would not be able to keep these promises.

BATTLE FOR LONG ISLAND

Meanwhile, a massive British fleet had been sighted off the coast of New York City. General Howe had returned. In the coming weeks, about thirty thousand British troops and German mercenaries landed on Staten Island, south of the city.

Britain's plan was to take control of New York Harbor, the Hudson River Valley, and Fort Ticonderoga. If successful, the British planned to move into Massachusetts and take control of the colony. With Massachusetts in their hands, the British were sure the other colonies would give up the rebellion.

General Howe shared command with General Guy Carleton, who was to attack from Quebec and move south. General Howe would capture New York City and march north to meet Carleton.

Washington had guessed the British strategy months earlier. So he had already moved much of his army to New York City, which lay at the southern tip of the island of Manhattan. Troops worked throughout the summer, building a series of forts to protect the city from invasion.

Washington hoped that with good preparation he could defeat the British forces, which greatly outnumbered his own. At most, the American general had only nineteen thousand men. And many of them were poorly equipped, poorly trained, and inexperienced militiamen. This force was not a match for the thirty thousand well-equipped, well-trained, and experienced British troops, cavalry (soldiers on horseback), and naval fleet with more than four hundred warships, twelve thousand guns, and ten thousand sailors.

The elaborate network of American forts surrounded the entire city. Washington also built two lines of defense on Long Island, an island across the East River from Manhattan. Running between the island's forested hills were passes (low-lying areas) that the Patriot troops were to defend. Washington hoped these two lines could stop the British from crossing the East River into New York City.

Even with these careful preparations, one of Washington's commanders had overlooked an area of Long Island's outer defenses. Most of the Patriot forces were guarding the western passes on Long Island. A pass to the east, the Jamaica Pass, was guarded by only a handful of American troops. A British spy shared this information with General Howe.

On August 22, 1776, Howe landed his forces on Long Island. Five days later, in a brilliant move, Howe sent part of his army to attack the heavily guarded western passes. His aim was to draw the Americans to the western end of the island.

The Patriots played right into Howe's hands. Unknown to the Americans, Howe had sent the larger part of his force through the Jamaica Pass the night before. This army swooped southward, behind the American positions. By 8:30 A.M. on August 27, Howe had surrounded much of the Patriot force. More than one thousand of Washington's troops were captured. Nearly as many were killed or wounded. The British suffered four hundred casualties (men either killed, wounded, or captured).

By noon, Howe had routed the Americans, who waited for an attack on the second line of defense. The attack never came. Ignoring the pleas of his officers, who

General Sir William Howe

General Sir William Howe (1729–1814) joined the British army at age seventeen and fought in the French and Indian War. His experiences in the colonies—getting to know, understand, and sympathize with Americans—would influence his attitude toward British actions against the Patriots. Howe held a seat in Parliament beginning in 1758. As relations between Britain and America soured, Howe often criticized his country's harsh policies against the colonies. A year before the Battles of Lexington and Concord, he said publicly that he doubted the "British Army could enforce" the laws George III and Parliament were creating to punish the colonies.

Howe has often been criticized for his handling of the war. Historians have pointed out that the general had several opportunities to crush the rebellion. Had he pursued the Americans farther after Bunker Hill, for example, he might have destroyed their entire army and the revolution with it. But Howe hoped to end the rebellion by defeating the Americans without destroying them. And his firsthand experience of the bloodbath at Bunker Hill—where he had personally led his soldiers—taught Howe that American fighters were not to be taken lightly.

The Battle of Long Island
August – September 1776

Legend:
- British Troops
- British Troop Movement
- British Ship
- Patriot Troops
- Patriot Troop Movement
- Hills
- City
- Fort
- Road
- Swamp

Miles
0   1   2
0   1   2   3
Kilometers

N

Fort Washington

Fort Lee

Battle of Harlem Heights, September 16

Long Island Sound

Hudson River

MANHATTAN

Patriot Retreat

British Advance

Hell's Gate

Kip's Bay

British Landing: September 15

Newtown Creek

WASHINGTON

NEW JERSEY

Paulus Hook

New York City

Fort George

East River

American Withdrawal: August 29

Brooklyn

LONG ISLAND

Jamaica Pass

Bedford

Heights of Guan

UPPER NEW YORK BAY

Fort Defiance

Gowanus Bay

Flatbush

HOWE 10,000

British Fleet

GRANT 5,000

Night March: August 26

Jamaica Bay

STATEN ISLAND

HOWE 32,000

Gravesend

LOWER NEW YORK BAY

claimed they could finish the war right then and there, Howe once again chose not to pursue the Americans. Instead, the British general ordered his men to dig in and wait.

General Washington took full advantage of Howe's decision. On August 29,

under cover of fog and nightfall, the 9,500 Americans slipped across the East River to New York City. Fearing that another British attack could surround and completely destroy his battle-weary army, the American general began moving his

New York City Ablaze

Washington's army had been unable to stop the British from taking New York. But the Americans did their best to make sure the city was as unlivable as possible. On the night of September 20, groups of Patriots set the city ablaze. About one-quarter of the city—some six hundred homes and buildings—were damaged by the huge fire. It had been set against the wishes of the Continental Congress, which did not want to see America's largest city damaged. Washington denied having ordered the fire. But he expressed pleasure with the outcome: "Some good honest fellow, has done more for us than we were disposed to do ourselves."

troops out of the city, leaving behind one-third of his men.

On September 15, 1776, British troops landed at Kip's Bay, on the east shore of Manhattan, north of New York City. The remaining American troops in New York quickly retreated. America's largest city had fallen to the British.

Howe's army did not stop there, however. British troops chased Washington's forces up Manhattan Island. British and American forces clashed at Harlem Heights on September 16, 1776, with the Americans scoring a much-needed victory. Weeks later, however, the British seized two American forts on the Hudson River, taking nearly three thousand prisoners, dozens of cannons, and many supplies.

On October 28, 1776, Washington's army was again routed at White Plains, north of New York City. The Americans then were forced to flee southward across the Hudson into New Jersey, where Howe continued to pursue them.

Retreating through New Jersey, the Americans tried to slow the British pursuit

After being routed at Long Island, Patriot troops were forced to flee across Gowanus Creek. Dozens were cut down by British musketfire as they struggled through the marshy waters.

by destroying bridges and blocking roads. By early December, Washington and what remained of his army had completed a humiliating retreat across New Jersey, setting up camp in Pennsylvania, on the western side of the Delaware River.

For Washington and the Patriots, the situation seemed hopeless. "If I were to wish the bitterest curse to an enemy...I should put him in my situation," Washington wrote in a letter to a cousin.

Believing he had crushed the Americans, Howe stationed some of his troops in different parts of New Jersey. Then he took most of his men with him to New York City to camp for the winter.

But Washington did receive some good news from his army in the north. The British had failed to invade the United States from Canada. While leading his troops southward across Lake Champlain in northern New York State, British general Carleton was confronted by a ragtag American fleet led by Benedict Arnold.

The two forces clashed on October 11 and 12, 1776. In bitter fighting, the British routed Arnold and his fleet, forcing the Americans to flee to nearby Fort Ticonderoga. But even with this victory, the battle stopped Carleton from continuing his invasion. The British general retreated to Canada for the winter.

Nathan Hale

Nathan Hale (1755–1776) was born in Coventry, Connecticut. He studied at Yale College and became a teacher, joining the Continental Army as a lieutenant. Promoted to the rank of captain, Hale earned the praise of his superiors when he and a small company of men stole a British supply ship. His courageous actions won him a spot in the Rangers, an American fighting unit that specialized in dangerous missions.

After the American defeat at Long Island, George Washington made a plea for spies. The general needed information on British troop movements. Hale volunteered. Disguising himself as a teacher, Hale wandered through the British army camp in New York City. The British had just taken the city and were on the lookout for suspicious characters. Hale's athletic build and Connecticut accent caught their attention. They searched him, finding maps and other documents that made it clear he was a spy.

General Howe ordered Hale to be hanged. Legend has it that as the noose was being placed around his neck, someone asked Hale if he had anything to say. With courage and dignity, the twenty-one-year-old Hale is said to have replied, "I only regret that I have but one life to lose for my country."

SOLDIERS AND UNIFORMS

The American Soldier Although many upper-class Patriot men joined the army, a large percentage of those who served came from the poorest of society. Some joined the army for adventure. Others enlisted to escape debt, jail, or unwanted obligations. Some were outcasts. A few were even deserters from the British army. Most were poor. For these men, the enlistment bounty (payment) and the promise of food, shelter, and pay were worth the risk of death or injury in battle.

Beginning in 1776, the Continental Congress promised new recruits money, land, and an annual allowance for clothing. However, the financially strapped congress was rarely able to keep these promises. Even decades after the war ended, American officers and soldiers were still waiting for the land and money they had been promised years earlier.

The Continental Army started as an untried, unruly group of citizen militiamen. Through training and discipline, Washington forged an effective fighting force. This force often surprised the British with its toughness in battle.

The Continental Army Uniform Because of lack of money, few Continental Army soldiers had uniforms during the early years of the war. Most wore civilian (everyday) clothes or deerskin hunting shirts and breeches (short trousers). The soldiers' rugged duties tended to wear out their clothes quickly. Completely uniformed units were an exception.

A Continental soldier

The Continental Army never had a consistent look. At the beginning of the war, American soldiers wore brown long coats with white waistcoats (vests) and breeches. In later years, the more familiar dark blue long coats were issued. Throughout the war, gray, green, and even red coats were worn by different units. The color of lapels also varied among red, white, green, gray, blue, and buff. The color often depended on the regiment's home state. Most soldiers wore cocked (three-cornered) hats like the soldier above is wearing.

The American soldier's equipment included his musket and bayonet, as well as a cartridge box. This box held his supply of premade cartridges—each containing a musket ball and a one-shot supply of gunpowder. The soldier carried the rest of his equipment—eating utensils, food, water, and a blanket—in a knapsack slung over his shoulder.

The British Soldier Life in the British army was difficult. For most British soldiers, service meant traveling overseas to colonies in America, India, and the West Indies. In the colonies, the population often resented the soldiers' presence. Pay was low and discipline was harsh. Given these circumstances, it is not surprising George III had a difficult time recruiting men to serve in America. Early in 1776, he was forced to hire mercenaries from German states to fill the British ranks.

Many British soldiers, like their American counterparts, came from the bottom of the social ladder. Some were criminals who had been given the choice of service or prison. Others were simply taken from their homes and forced to serve, although this practice was illegal. British soldiers were well trained. The tough discipline imposed on them made them strong and effective fighters. British forces won the majority of the battles fought against Americans.

The British Army Uniform British soldiers were expected to "look like a picture." If a British soldier wasn't properly dressed, he could be whipped. British uniforms were made of canvas and wool. They were heavy and hot and took a long time to put on properly. The typical red long coat was decorated with lace, buttons, and piping. Not all units wore red coats. Some dressed in green, blue, gray, or yellow. Different units also wore different colored lapels, including yellow, white, blue, buff, and red. Two belts made an X across a soldier's uniform *(left)*. One belt held his bayonet, the other his cartridge box. Each trooper carried a knapsack and other gear, often totaling about sixty pounds. The combination of the sometimes hot American climate (especially during the war's southern campaigns), tight woolen clothes, and heavy burdens made long marches brutal.

A British soldier

Defeated Hessian troops line up to surrender to American forces after the Battle of Trenton. Colonel Rall, the Hessian commander, was killed in the fighting.

WASHINGTON CROSSES THE DELAWARE

To give his soldiers—and the revolution itself—some hope, Washington designed a bold plan for the surprise attack on Trenton, New Jersey. With the help of a clever American spy, Washington gathered information about the enemy force across the Delaware River. The city was occupied by a unit of Hessians, some of the German mercenaries hired by George III. The American general learned that the German troops had done little to set up a defense of the city. If Washington could catch the Hessians off guard, he might be able to deliver the victory he so desperately needed. And what better time to surprise the enemy than the day after Christmas, when it was hoped the Hessians would be sleeping off their celebration?

Washington's plan had great potential. But after a slow and treacherous river crossing and a long march down frozen roads, the troops were weary and cold. As the soldiers approached Trenton, they realized that most of their muskets were too wet to fire.

Still, the Americans unleashed their assault at 8:00 A.M., catching the Hessians off guard. By 9:30 A.M., the battle was over, and the Americans had captured more than nine hundred prisoners and seized desperately needed supplies. For the first time in months, the Patriots celebrated a victory. But would this glimmer of hope be enough to inspire Washington's worn-out troops to continue? Without reenlistments, the revolution had no hope of continuing.

> EYEWITNESS QUOTE:
> THE DELAWARE RIVER
>
> "I never have seen Washington so determined as he is now. He stands on the bank of the river, wrapped in his cloak, superintending the landing of his troops. He is calm and collected, but very determined. The storm is changing to sleet, and cuts like a knife. The last cannon is being landed, and we are ready to mount our horses."
>
> —an American officer

THE TURNING POINT

5

After the victory at Trenton, Washington hoped he could convince his soldiers to reenlist. Mounted on his horse in front of his army, the general gave a stiff request to continue the fight. No one stepped forward to volunteer. Then Washington spoke again—this time from his heart.

"You have done all I asked you to do, and more than could be reasonably expected, but your country is at stake, your wives, your houses, and all that you hold dear. You have worn yourselves out with fatigues and hardships, but we know not how to spare you. If you will consent to stay only one month longer, you will render that service to the cause of liberty, and to your country, which you probably never can do under any other circumstance."

An awkward silence followed. Then, "to a man," his troops stepped forward and reenlisted.

Days later, Washington and his men went on the offensive again. Outraged by the defeat at Trenton, General Howe sent troops from New York City to crush the American army. Washington learned that five thousand British troops, under

General Cornwallis

the command of General Cornwallis, were headed his way. Another 1,200 redcoats had been left in the town of Princeton to guard the rear of Cornwallis's force.

Knowing that his exhausted troops stood no chance against Cornwallis's army, Washington resorted to trickery. In the dark of the night of January 1, 1777, the American general marched most of his army out of Trenton. Washington left behind only four hundred men, with orders to make the British believe the entire American army was present. Setting up makeshift campsites, the four hundred remaining Patriot soldiers kept hundreds of campfires burning throughout the night. Cooking smells and loud voices carried across the nighttime air. They scraped shovels on the ground, leading the British to think that the Patriots

were digging trenches and preparing for a battle the next morning.

Meanwhile, Washington led a silent march around the flank (side) of Cornwallis's army. Quickly they marched past Cornwallis to Princeton, where they descended on the smaller British force. The strategy worked brilliantly. The British were forced to retreat, giving the Patriots yet another victory and control of most of New Jersey.

BRITAIN'S MILITARY STRATEGY FOR 1777

After the Princeton victory, both the British and the American armies retired to their winter encampments. Washington and his men settled at Morristown, New Jersey.

> EYEWITNESS QUOTE:
> BATTLE OF PRINCETON
>
> " . . . the [enemy's] fire was dreadful and three balls [bullets] . . . had grazed me; one passed within my elbow nicking my great coat and carried away the breech of Sergeant McKnatts gun, he being close behind me, another carried away the inside edge of one of my shoesoles, another had [nicked] my hat and indeed they seemed as thick as hail."
>
> —Captain Thomas Rodney, American militia

Continental Army troops attack British forces at Princeton. Washington's risky surprise attacks gave the Americans some desperately needed victories.

WINTER ENCAMPMENTS

In the 1700s, most armies did not fight during the winter. This was due to the dangers of cold weather and the difficulty of movement during the freezing winter months. Instead, military forces spent that time in camps resting, training, and preparing for spring and summer battles to come.

Britain's military strategy for 1777 was to win control of New York. Control of New York State would allow Britain to isolate the New England states from the rest of America. If they controlled New England, British leaders believed, they would again control America.

The campaign called for a three-pronged attack to meet in Albany, in northern New York. General John Burgoyne was to carry out a British invasion from Canada. General Howe was to sail up the Hudson River from New York City. Lieutenant Colonel Barry St. Leger was to march his troops eastward from Lake Ontario. Along the way, the three forces would crush Washington's army.

Burgoyne began his part of the British campaign in June 1777. With an army of 9,500 men and 138 cannons, he attacked Fort Ticonderoga. The 2,300 Patriot troops guarding the fort were outnumbered, weary, and sick. The Patriots abandoned Fort Ticonderoga on July 5.

General Burgoyne chased the Patriots southward along the Hudson River. Too weak to stop and fight the British troops, the American force did its best to slow them down. They chopped down trees, dug ditches, destroyed bridges, and dammed (blocked) creeks. The Americans also destroyed all food, livestock, and crops in their path to make sure Burgoyne's thousands of marching men would find nothing to eat. These scorched-earth tactics, as they were called, were successful in slowing the British pursuit.

With his army starving, Burgoyne sent a force of one thousand German mercenaries to find food and supplies. On August 16, 1777, 1,600 New England militiamen, led by General John Stark, ambushed (surprised) the Germans near the town of Bennington, Vermont. A fierce battle followed. By the time it ended, only one hundred mercenaries returned to their commander.

Patriot colonel John Stark addresses his troops before the Battle of Bennington. In his rousing speech, he said, "There are the redcoats and they are ours, or Molly Stark [the American general's wife] sleeps a widow tonight."

By late summer, General Burgoyne's army was in tatters and needed reinforcement from General Howe. But Howe was busy planning an invasion of Philadelphia, the seat of the Continental Congress. By seizing the city, Howe was hoping to make up for his defeats at Trenton and Princeton. He also hoped to meet and destroy Washington's army in one final battle.

BATTLES OF BRANDYWINE CREEK AND GERMANTOWN

In July General Howe sailed southward from New York with eighteen thousand troops. Washington had suspected Howe would make an attempt on Philadelphia. When he heard the news of Howe's departure from New York, the American general quickly made plans to defend the city.

Washington set up his defense along Brandywine Creek, southwest of Phila-

---

EYEWITNESS QUOTE: BENNINGTON, VERMONT

"[T]he scene which . . . [followed] defies all power of language to describe. The bayonet, the butt of the rifle, the saber [sword], the pike were in full play; and men fell, as they rarely fall in modern war. . . ."

—a German officer

---

delphia. Here the British would only be able to cross the creek in certain shallow areas. Washington placed his men along eight fords (shallow crossing places), with his strongest force positioned at Chadd's Ford, where the British were most likely to cross. He scattered smaller units in a six-mile line along the creek.

On September 11, 1777, Howe and his men advanced on the American positions at Brandywine Creek. The British general used the same strategy that had worked so successfully on Long Island. Howe sent half his troops to meet Washington's main force at Chadd's Ford. At the same time, Howe ordered the rest of his men to swing around and surprise the right flank of Washington's army.

Howe's tactic worked brilliantly. After a day of furious fighting, Washington was forced to retreat, with about 1,300 casualties. This was more than twice the number of British losses. A week later, the Continental Congress fled Philadelphia, and on September 26, British troops marched into the American capital.

But, once again, Howe did not immediately follow up his victory and try to crush the Continental Army. Instead, the British general maneuvered around the countryside beyond Philadelphia, hoping to trap Washington. Washington and his men were able to avoid head-to-head battles. By early September, Howe had set up camp at Germantown,

Baggage Trains

The British army was dependent on baggage trains. These consisted of hundreds of carts hauling artillery and the supplies and belongings of the officers and soldiers. A baggage train for a large British army could be miles long. Such massive amounts of equipment and the difficulties of moving them greatly slowed down the army's movements. In addition, these supply lines were vulnerable to attack by American forces.

At the Battle of Brandywine Creek, Washington received conflicting reports about the size and location of British troops. By the time he had learned the truth, the British had gained the advantage.

Pennsylvania, five miles outside of Philadelphia.

Washington planned a daring surprise attack on Howe's men at Germantown. He divided his eleven thousand troops into columns (groups), each under a different commanding officer. Washington hoped to encircle Howe's encampment and rout the British and German troops, forcing them to surrender.

On the morning of October 4, 1777, the Americans approached the British camp through dense fog. Washington's complicated battle plan quickly fell apart, due to the fog and lack of communication among the columns. Even worse, more than one hundred British troops had barricaded themselves inside a house built of stone blocks. From here, the British soldiers picked off the unprotected American troops with musketfire.

The Americans battered the house with cannonballs, but nothing seemed to blast through its stone walls. Billows of smoke added to the fog-filled sky. In the fog and confusion, two American units began firing at each other. Unable to gain the advantage on the British, Washington led his remaining troops on another humiliating retreat. More than one thousand men had been lost to death, injury, or capture.

EYEWITNESS QUOTE:
BRANDYWINE CREEK

"Cannon balls flew thick and many and small arms soared like the rolling of a drum."

—an American commander

WEAPONS OF THE AMERICAN REVOLUTION

The musket was the chief weapon used by soldiers on both sides during the war. During a typical battle, or engagement, soldiers stood shoulder to shoulder in two or three separate lines. As one line fired a volley (round of shots), the other line or lines reloaded their weapons. Usually, each side exchanged two to three volleys before engaging in hand-to-hand combat with bayonets. Other weapons used during the war included pistols, swords, rifles, knives, and artillery.

Americans tended to be more accurate with their firearms than their British counterparts. This was most likely because many Americans hunted for food and sport, giving them valuable experience in the use of rifles and muskets. In Britain, only the privileged classes were allowed to hunt, so most British soldiers did not have the chance to develop good marksmanship.

Musket Every American militiaman was expected to own a musket or rifle. Muskets were not very accurate, and most could not be counted on to hit their mark past fifty yards.

A musket

Rifle A rifle looks much like a musket. The major difference between the two weapons is the inside of the rifle's barrel. It is rifled, meaning it has grooves to make the ball spin as it shoots out. Rifling makes a gun much more accurate at longer distances. A good rifle in the hands of a good marksman could accurately hit targets from three hundred yards.

Balls

Balls American and British muskets fired three-quarter-inch balls. These projectiles packed a wallop. They broke bones and ripped open large flesh wounds. Musket balls were made by pouring hot lead into a mold.

Ball and Powder Cartridge Cartridges were the early versions of modern bullets. The cartridge combined gunpowder and ball for faster and easier loading. (Previously, loading a gun involved pouring powder inside the barrel and then inserting the ball.) Cartridges were stored in a pack called a cartridge box.

A bayonet

Bayonet A bayonet was attached to the end of a rifle or musket. Bayonets were used during hand-to-hand fighting. They were also crucial as backup weapons when wet weather made flints and gunpowder too damp to fire.

Sword Officers usually carried a sword or saber, which were used both as weapons and as means of signaling troops. Wealthier officers often owned sabers with highly detailed etchings and designs.

Pistol Some officers carried a pistol or a pair of pistols (small handguns). Wealthier officers often owned beautiful custom-made pistols.

Artillery Artillery is the term used for cannons and other heavy guns. Cannons fired a variety of different projectiles.

Shot Cannonballs were round (to make them fly straight and far) and made of solid iron. They weren't very useful against troops but could knock down forts and other structures.

Shot

Shells These were hollow balls loaded with explosives. A fuse was used to time the explosive for maximum effect. For example, a shell could be shot into a group of infantry with the fuse set to explode shortly after it landed, causing many injuries. When attacking a fort, soldiers could set a fuse to explode in midair, causing a rain of hot debris to fall on the occupiers.

Grapeshot This was a mass of projectiles that scattered after leaving the cannon. Scattershot was often used on groups of infantry with lethal results.

Loading a cannon

During the Battle of Germantown, a unit of British troops turned a mansion into a fortress. Dozens of Americans were killed in a fruitless assault on the building.

BATTLE OF SARATOGA

While Howe and Washington were battling for Philadelphia, General Burgoyne and his weary army were continuing their invasion from the north. As Burgoyne's army marched south toward Albany, its path was blocked by an American force at Bemis Heights, just south of Saratoga, New York. The soldiers who had abandoned Fort Ticonderoga had gathered there with other American troops to join a growing army under General Horatio Gates. News of the Patriot victory at Bennington, Vermont, had brought local militias flocking to join the army under Gates's command.

By mid-September, Burgoyne's situation had become desperate. Wanting to march on to Albany, the British general decided to attack the Americans at Bemis Heights. On September 19, 1777, a force of 4,200 British, German, and Loyalist troops advanced on the Americans. Burgoyne's men were met by a ferocious American charge, led by Generals Benedict Arnold and Daniel Morgan. After a day of bloody fighting, the Americans retreated to Bemis Heights. The British had held their ground, but at a terrible cost—six hundred killed, wounded, or captured.

Two days later, Burgoyne received news that a British force of three thousand men under General Henry Clinton had left New York City to come to his aid. Burgoyne's troops settled in and waited for these reinforcements. But Clinton made slow progress

Benedict Arnold *(center, on horse)* suffered a broken leg during a charge at the second battle at Saratoga. But his aggressive leadership helped win the day for the Americans.

up the well-defended Hudson River. Three weeks passed with no sign of relief. The weary Burgoyne faced a difficult decision. Should he launch another attack on Bemis Heights or retreat? Although heavily outnumbered, Burgoyne chose to fight.

On October 7, 1777, Burgoyne launched his attack. The Americans were ready and quickly pushed the British back behind their line of defense. Seeing the opportunity to break Burgoyne's army, Benedict Arnold gathered his troops for a frenzied assault on the battered British defenses. During one charge, a musket ball broke Arnold's leg, knocking him out of action. But by nightfall, Burgoyne's army was on the run, leaving a few supplies, guns, and ammunition.

After trudging through mud and rain, Burgoyne tried to set up a new line of defense. But more American troops were coming into the area. Soon the Americans had surrounded the starving British army. With no hope of escape, General Burgoyne

and his 5,800 troops surrendered on October 17, 1777.

AN HISTORIC VICTORY

The British surrender at Saratoga was felt throughout the world. For the first time,

Benedict Arnold's Charge

Benedict Arnold's bold actions at the second battle at Saratoga made him a national hero. Interestingly, he never should have been on the battlefield in the first place. A fiery personality, Arnold frequently clashed with his commander, General Horatio Gates. After a series of personal disputes following the first battle at Saratoga, Gates stripped Arnold of his command and ordered him to remain in his tent. But when the second battle began, Arnold refused to sit out the fight. Disobeying orders, he mounted his horse, charged into the battle, and helped lead the Americans to victory.

France, Britain's greatest enemy, realized that the American rebellion stood a good chance of succeeding. Early on, the French had seen an opportunity to get revenge for their defeats in the French and Indian War and other wars against Britain. They had been providing secret aid—in the form of weapons, supplies, and money—to the Americans since 1776. But they had yet to commit any troops or ships to the American cause.

News of the American victory reached France in early December. The American ambassadors to France—Benjamin Franklin, Silas Deane, and Arthur Lee—immediately began negotiating an alliance, or partnership in war, with France. On February 5, 1778, France and the United States signed a treaty of alliance. A few months later, French ships attacked British vessels off the coast of Britain. The war had expanded to global proportions.

Benjamin Franklin

Benjamin Franklin (1706–1790) was a writer, journalist, editor, publisher, postmaster, scientist, inventor, diplomat, and the most famous American of his time. Born the fifteenth of seventeen children, in Boston, Massachusetts, Franklin attended school for only two years. At age ten, his father put him to work in the family's candle and soap making shop. During his free time, he learned writing, geometry, algebra, navigation, logic, grammar, and the various disciplines of science. He also studied French, German, Italian, Latin, and Spanish.

Franklin's experiments with electricity made him famous throughout America and Europe. His many inventions include the lightning rod, bifocal glasses, and the Franklin stove (an efficient furnace).

While in Great Britain as a diplomat for the colonies (1757–1775), Franklin observed the crumbling relations between America and the mother country. Returning to America shortly after the Battles of Lexington and Concord, he was appointed as a delegate to the Second Continental Congress. He played an important role in the drafting and ratification of the Declaration of Independence.

Because of his brilliance and his popularity in Europe, Franklin was the obvious choice to represent the new United States in negotiations with France. His homespun wit, courtesy, and modesty made him a symbol of America for many French. From the moment of his arrival in Paris, he was treated as a celebrity.

A LONG AND DEADLY WINTER

6

As negotiations were taking place between France and the United States, the British and American armies were encamped for the winter. General Howe and his troops spent the winter of 1777–1778 enjoying the comforts of Philadelphia. Washington and his troops were camped twenty miles to the northeast, in the freezing countryside of Valley Forge, Pennsylvania. While the British enjoyed food and shelter, the Continental Army faced the bitter winter elements.

As cold weather set in, Washington's troops had to build their own barracks (living quarters). Washington could have easily moved into a home nearby or taken possession of the first barrack that was built. But he refused to do this, telling his men, "I will share in your hardships and partake of every inconvenience." Not until after his men were properly sheltered did Washington take up residence in a nearby house.

Conditions at Valley Forge were terrible. Many soldiers were dressed only in worn rags. Blankets were badly needed. Deadly diseases such as smallpox and typhoid fever struck many of the troops. Food was in short supply. Men survived on firecakes and pepper hot soup. Firecakes were patties of flour and water baked on hot stones. Pepper hot soup was water cooked with a thin strip of tripe (stomach lining of a cow) and flavored with a handful of peppercorns. By the spring of 1778, nearly

Valley Forge Huts

The American soldiers at Valley Forge built their own huts, using trees from the surrounding countryside. Each hut was sixteen feet long, fourteen feet wide, and six and one-half feet high. A single hut housed twelve soldiers. Each had a small stone fireplace for heating and cooking. Bunk beds were made with wooden slats, which were covered with straw mats when available. Blankets were a luxury few men enjoyed.

one-fourth of Washington's army had died of disease or starvation.

Somehow, Washington's army survived the winter—and even emerged a stronger, more disciplined force. For this improvement, the Americans could thank a German officer, Friedrich Wilhelm Augustus von Steuben, who had arrived at Valley Forge in February. Baron von Steuben, a native of the kingdom of Prussia (in the northern region of modern-day Germany), was an experienced soldier who understood the importance of discipline.

The energetic officer drastically improved the Continental Army's training methods. He spent weeks drilling the American soldiers in the ways of the Prussian army. Through strict attention to discipline and details, he helped to mold the army into a hardened fighting force. His efforts earned him the title "the first teacher of the American army."

Baron von Steuben drills troops at Valley Forge. His efforts would pay off in battles to come.

Baron von Steuben

Von Steuben once shared his training philosophy: "[A Captain's] first object should be to gain the love of his men by treating them with every possible kindness and humanity, inquiring into their complaints and when well founded, seeing them redressed. He should know every man of his company by name and character. He should often visit those who are sick, speak tenderly to them, see that the public provision, whether of medicine or diet, is duly administered, and procure them besides such comforts and medicines as are in his power."

By the spring of 1778, food, clothing, and other supplies began to trickle into the American camp. Those who had survived the winter at Valley Forge came out as part of a disciplined, highly trained army. When news of the alliance with France arrived on May 5, the morale (attitude) of the American troops soared. Victory seemed within reach.

France's entry into the war forced Britain to change its strategy. Unlike the Americans, the French had a large navy. The British could no longer take for granted their mastery of the waterways of North America. To better defend themselves against France's naval threat, the British decided to gather their forces in New York.

Sir Henry Clinton replaced General Howe as commander in chief in the spring of 1778. His orders were to evacuate Philadelphia. Clinton and his army of ten thousand British soldiers and three thousand Loyalists began their march northward to New York in mid-June. Two days later, Washington received word of Clinton's evacuation. The American general didn't want to risk a major battle against a force that equaled his own. So he and his generals decided to follow and harass Clinton's troops. Along the way, the Americans would look for a chance to make a major attack.

BATTLE OF MONMOUTH

On June 28, 1778, the Americans clashed with Clinton's forces at Monmouth, New Jersey. In searing temperatures that hovered near 100°F, the two armies fought throughout the day. One soldier recorded it as "the most scorching summer day ever known in America." Both sides suffered hundreds of casualties, but neither was able to gain the upper hand. The battle ended without a clear winner. That night, Clinton and his

Molly Pitcher

Molly Pitcher was the nickname given to a number of women who showed courage in battle. The most famous of them was Mary Ludwig Hayes, the wife of a Pennsylvania artillery crewman. Mary was a camp follower. She accompanied her husband and his army at camp and on the march. During the Battle of Monmouth, she braved enemy fire to bring pitchers of water to her husband's thirsty unit, earning the name Molly Pitcher. When her spouse fell wounded, Mary took over for him.

A soldier who witnessed Mary's actions described her remarkable bravery. "While in the act of reaching for a cartridge, a cannon shot from the enemy passed directly between her legs without doing any other damage than carrying away all the lower part of her petticoat. Looking at it with apparent unconcern, she observed it was lucky it did not pass a little higher, for in that case it might have carried away something else." Her efforts were rewarded with a sergeant's warrant, which entitled her to a sergeant's pay and allowances. Mary's tombstone in the old Carlisle cemetery in Pennsylvania describes her as the Heroine of Monmouth.

army withdrew from the field and continued their march to New York.

Monmouth was the longest battle of the American Revolution and the last major battle fought in the north. For the rest of the war, the British would focus most of their efforts on the southern states and the western frontier.

WAR ON THE FRONTIER

Throughout the war, the majority of the fighting took place within the thirteen colonies. But the more sparsely populated western frontier also saw violence—often of a very brutal kind.

George III's Proclamation of 1763 had sought to avoid conflict with Native Americans by forbidding colonists from settling west of the Appalachian Mountains. Yet white settlers ignored the proclamation and continued to move onto Indian lands, angering many Native Americans.

Fighting on the frontier was often merciless. In July 1778, a group of about one thousand Loyalists and Indians set out from Fort Niagara on Lake Ontario to the Wyoming Valley in western Pennsylvania. This raiding party descended on the Patriot settlers of the area, killing hundreds of people—many of them women and children—and destroying hundreds of homes. Such raids continued through the summer and fall, leaving hundreds dead and terrorizing the frontier population.

The Patriot response came the following year. In July 1779, General Washington sent a force of four thousand men under General John Sullivan to punish the Iroquois Indians. Sullivan's army marched through the frontier, destroying forty Iroquois villages and burning thousands of acres of crops and orchards. Most of the Indians chose to flee rather than try to fight the huge American army, so nearly all of the villages were empty when Sullivan's troops arrived. But the destruction of their homes and food crippled the Iroquois. Washington thought these retaliatory attacks would convince the Indians to stay out of the war. But the raids only inspired the Iroquois to seek revenge the following year with more raids on American settlements.

The Western Frontier

Farther west, a young soldier from Virginia named George Rogers Clark led a small party of Patriots through the western frontier, the area that later became the states of Kentucky, Illinois, Indiana, Ohio, Michigan, and Wisconsin. Clark's goal was to capture Britain's Fort Detroit, near Lake Erie.

George Rogers Clark

Marching through Indian territory was dangerous, and Clark only managed to recruit about 175 men for the mission. This tiny army sailed west on the Ohio River into the frontier in June 1778. Clark's first goal was the British outpost at Kaskaskia, about fifty miles southeast of St. Louis. On July 4, Clark and his men took the fort without firing a shot. Clark's men also captured outposts farther north at Cahokia and Vincennes.

Clark's activity caught the attention of Hamilton, who set out from Fort Detroit in October 1778 to recapture the towns and their forts for the British. With such a small army at his command, Clark had no way to properly defend his conquests. For this reason, Hamilton easily recaptured Vincennes in December.

MEDICAL CARE

More soldiers—six out of seven—who died in the American Revolution died from diseases rather than from wounds received in battle. The germ theory—the idea that many diseases are caused by tiny microorganisms called bacteria—had not yet been developed. Neither doctors nor their patients understood that cleanliness and a well-balanced diet were crucial in fighting disease. Surgeons did not wash themselves, their equipment, or their patients before surgery. As a result, nearly half of all surgical patients died from infection. This ignorance—combined with crowded, dirty living conditions, lack of proper clothing, and severe food shortages—made the army camp a perfect home for deadly diseases such as typhoid, typhus, and smallpox.

Doctor Training The vast majority of American doctors had learned their trade through apprenticeships, in which they worked for an experienced doctor. In most such cases, the master had little or no formal medical training, either. In the larger American cities, some medical students had the chance to go to lectures given by formally educated doctors. Yet even the best-trained physicians of the time had flawed theories about how the human body worked and healed. Their treatments were often more harmful than the disease or injury itself. As one medical historian and doctor wrote, "The Revolutionary soldier had an enemy he had not counted upon—symptomatic treatment by his physician."

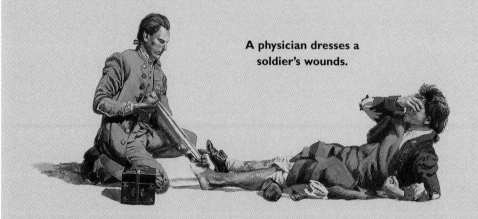

A physician dresses a soldier's wounds.

Surgeries Drugs to kill pain or ether to put patients asleep were unknown at the time. At best, the unfortunate soldier might be given a shot of whiskey and a lead ball to chew on to keep from screaming and biting his tongue. Usually the patient was held down on the operating table by his comrades as he writhed in agony. Surgeons performed three basic operations.

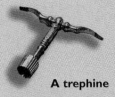

A trephine

- *Trephining* This was a popular method for treating head wounds. Using a corkscrew-like instrument called a trephine, the surgeon drilled a hole in the patient's skull. This was done to release pressure on the brain due to swelling and fluid buildup.

- *Amputation* The surgeon sawed off the damaged limb. The stump was covered in a layer of lint and a layer of linen.

A surgeon's saw

- *Removing balls and shrapnel* Usually the surgeon tried to dig the foreign object out using his (unwashed) fingers. If the ball or piece of shell was beyond his reach, he might use a pair of tonglike forceps to grasp it.

Remedies In the late 1700s, many doctors' theories were based on ancient Greek concepts. These theories revolved around the body's fluids—blood, bile (a liquid produced by the liver), and phlegm (thick, sticky mucous secreted by an unhealthy respiratory system). The Greeks believed that when these fluids fell out of balance, disease flourished. They used the following remedies in hopes of achieving a healthy balance. Such treatments usually left the patient weaker or sicker than before.

- *Purging* Doctors mixed a variety of potions to purge a patient through vomiting or diarrhea. It was believed that purging would get rid of the sickness. But in many cases, the loss of fluids left the patient in much worse condition.

- *Blistering* This procedure involved mixing and applying a solution that made the skin blister. Doctors believed the blister drew the disease out of the body. When the blister was popped, the disease was released. In fact, the open wounds created by the blisters were prone to infection.

- *Bleeding/bloodletting* Doctors of the Revolutionary era believed that draining blood from the patient helped to combat disease. Since the blood was thought to be tainted with illness, removal of some of it was believed to be beneficial. As was the case with other remedies, the loss of blood only weakened the patient at a time when strength was badly needed to fight illness.

In early February, Clark went out to take Vincennes once again. After a grueling seventeen-day march in winter conditions, Clark and his 127 men arrived at the outskirts of the small town. On February 23, Clark's soldiers—many of them crack shots—began firing on the fort. They shot into openings through which cannons and rifles were fired. The Patriot sharpshooters picked off so many of Hamilton's men that by the next morning the fort's cannons were unmanned. Hamilton surrendered the next day.

Clark had regained control of nearly the entire area that would one day become the state of Illinois. But a lack of funds and volunteers kept him from achieving his goal to move on and conquer Fort Detroit.

THE WAR AT SEA

Early in the war, the Continental Congress established the Continental Navy, ordering the construction of a few warships. The congress also called for the conversion of a handful of merchant vessels into warships. But the small U.S. fleet never came close to challenging Britain's huge assortment of 270 vessels.

Early in the war, Britain took advantage of its dominance of the American coastline to block supplies from reaching the colonies. British warships also terrorized Patriot coastal towns by bombarding them with cannonfire.

Like many governments of the time, the Continental Congress hired privateers (pirates) to harass British shipping. Privateer

The American *Bonhomme Richard* defeated the British *Serapis* in a vicious battle in 1779.

The U.S. Navy's First Hero

John Paul Jones (1747–1792) was born John Paul in Kirkcudbrightshire, Scotland. He first went to sea at age twelve. By his mid-twenties, he was captaining ships. In 1773 he killed one of his men in what may have been self-defense. Fearing a charge of murder, the young captain fled to America.

After changing his name to John Paul Jones to hide his identity, he joined the new Continental Navy in December 1775. Jones spent much of the war lurking off the British Isles, attacking and capturing British merchant ships.

Jones's greatest battle was fought on the night of September 23, 1779. Jones and his squadron (group of ships) attacked a British merchant fleet off the coast of Britain. Jones's vessel, the *Bonhomme Richard* engaged in combat with the British warship *Serapis*. In a battle that lasted about four hours, the two vessels battered one another with cannonfire, gunshots, and grenades. Both ships caught fire. Jones rammed the *Serapis* and lashed the two vessels together.

The crews then engaged in deadly hand-to-hand combat. Nearly half of Jones's 380 sailors were killed, and the *Bonhomme Richard* began to take on water. But when the captain of the *Serapis* asked Jones if he was ready to surrender, the American replied, "I have not yet begun to fight!" At one point, one of the *Bonhomme Richard*'s crew tossed a grenade that ignited some of the *Serapis*'s gunpowder, causing a massive explosion. The British ship surrendered, and Jones assumed command while the *Bonhomme Richard* sank.

vessels were given permission by their government to attack and seize enemy ships. Once a ship had been commandeered (seized), its stolen cargo was then sold. The entire privateer crew received a percentage of the sale of the loot, with the Continental Congress receiving half of all profits.

Such actions benefited the American cause in several ways. The seizing of British goods—including weapons, ammunition, clothing, and food—kept such items out of British hands. In turn, these valuable supplies, as well as the captured ships themselves, usually went to Patriots. In addition, the threat created by privateers forced British warships to spend much of their time policing sea routes instead of attacking American targets. All in all, the Continental Congress hired two thousand privateer vessels during the war. These ships captured some three thousand British vessels and millions of dollars in cargo.

THE BRITISH MOVE SOUTH

George III and Parliament believed that most citizens in the southern states were still loyal to Britain. They reasoned that a British invasion of the south would bring out these Loyalists to support them. The Loyalists could then hold each area that the British gained, allowing the army to move on and conquer other Patriot strongholds. After gaining control of the south, British troops could again march on the northern states and finally crush the revolution.

Conquering Savannah, Georgia—a port city for the British navy—was the first order of business. A large force sailed from New York City into the mouth of the Savannah River in December 1778. It quickly captured the city and its port. The British then marched north to Augusta, Georgia, taking control of the state's capital city. By early 1779, Georgia had fallen into British hands.

French navy admiral Charles d'Estaing and Continental Army general Benjamin Lincoln tried to regain Savannah for the Americans in early September. D'Estaing's fleet sailed into the Savannah River carrying four thousand troops. The French admiral easily landed his men, who were soon joined by Lincoln's force of more than one thousand.

Were it not for a mistake on his part, d'Estaing might have easily taken Savannah. But instead of immediately marching on the city with his army, the admiral sent a demand for its surrender. This demand gave the British and the Loyalists time to set up a defense of the city. By the time the French and American forces finally invaded on October 9, 1779, the British and the Loyalists were ready for them. The attack proved to be a disaster for the French and the Americans, who suffered more than 1,100 casualties.

Eleven days later, d'Estaing loaded his troops back onto their ships and sailed out

After the French and American assault on Savannah failed, the British and the Loyalists counterattacked. The American troops were pushed into a nearby swamp and suffered heavy casualties.

At the Battle of Camden, inexperienced militiamen fled at the sight of charging British troops.

of Savannah, returning to France. General Lincoln marched his troops northward to Charleston, South Carolina, a city where another British invasion seemed likely.

A COUNTRY "LAID WASTE"

Encouraged by his victories in Georgia, General Clinton set his sights on South Carolina. On April 1, 1780, backed by warships and an army of more than ten thousand troops, Clinton surrounded the city. General Lincoln, in command of the American forces within Charleston, quickly realized he would not be able to stop Clinton's army. On April 19, he suggested surrendering to the British, but the citizens of Charleston refused to give in.

Weeks passed, with British and Loyalist troops moving closer to the city. On the night of May 9, the British started firing "hot shot"—grapeshot that had been heated red-hot—on the city. Several houses caught fire. Afraid of losing their homes, the townspeople changed their minds and urged Lincoln to give in to the British.

On May 12, Lincoln surrendered Charleston and his 5,500-man army to General Clinton. With thousands of Patriot troops captured, the south was wide open for the British to sweep through. Clinton left General Cornwallis in charge of British operations and returned to his headquarters in New York City.

The Continental Congress appointed General Horatio Gates to replace Lincoln. Washington did not agree with this decision—he favored one of his closest aides, Nathanael Greene. But Gates had impressed the congress with his leadership at the Battle of Saratoga. He had gone out of his way to make sure he received the majority of credit for that stunning victory. Gates had played an important role at Saratoga, but he had not actually participated in combat.

Gates marched south with orders to attack the British at Camden, South

Carolina. Local militia joined Gates's force along the way, building up the general's strength to four thousand troops. Cornwallis received word of Gates's approach and sent out a large army to meet the Americans. The two armies were marching on the same road toward each other. On the night of August 15, 1780, they collided.

After a short, confused battle in the dark, the two sides held their fire until sunrise. When dawn arrived, the British attacked, and half the American army collapsed and retreated. The Americans who held their line fought back as best they could but were overwhelmed by the British assault. In one day of combat, Gates's army was destroyed. About nine hundred American soldiers were killed or

wounded. Another one thousand were captured by Cornwallis's troops.

Gates was not killed or captured. Instead, the general was one of the first to flee the scene, riding the fastest horse available. Riding throughout the day, he didn't stop until he had reached Charlotte, North Carolina, about sixty miles away. His cowardice at Camden destroyed his reputation as a general. Months later, Gates was replaced by Washington's original choice, Nathanael Greene.

After Camden, Cornwallis and his army turned their attention to North Carolina. He left groups of Loyalists in South Carolina to protect the British strongholds. But many southern Patriots refused to give up their fight for independence. Led by men such as Francis Marion, Andrew Pickens, and Thomas Sumter, bands of southern Patriots used guerrilla tactics. They roamed the countryside and swamps, setting up quick and deadly ambushes of British and Loyalist troops.

In response, the Loyalists destroyed Patriot homes and sometimes murdered Patriot families. Patriots took revenge by murdering Loyalists. The situation quickly descended into chaos. "The whole country is in danger of being laid waste by the [Patriots] and [Loyalists] who pursue each other with as much relentless fury as beasts of prey," wrote Nathanael Greene. The war had already lasted more than five bloody years, with no end in sight.

Horatio Gates

7 TREASON AND TRIUMPH

While fighting raged in the southern states, George Washington struggled to keep his army in the northern states together. Miserable living conditions and lack of pay threatened to break up the Continental Army. The Continental Congress was nearly bankrupt. Its pleas for funding from the individual states were being ignored. On several occasions in 1780 and 1781, American soldiers would be called upon to stop other American troops from deserting in large numbers.

General Washington received encouragement in July 1780, when a French army, under the command of Jean de Vimeur, Count de Rochambeau, arrived. But Rochambeau's force of six thousand troops and eight war-

ships was not large enough to carry out Washington's proposed plan to retake New York City from the British. In fact, the Continental Army was in such a sorry state that Washington didn't even let the French commander see his ragged American troops, let alone fight alongside them.

Then, in September 1780, the Continental Army was dealt another crippling blow. Benedict Arnold, the hero of Saratoga and Washington's best fighting general, turned traitor. The outspoken Arnold, who was commander of the Patriot fort at West Point, had been planning to hand over this crucial outpost on the Hudson River to the British. In exchange, he would get a large sum of money. Arnold's treason was discovered before his plan was put into action, and he escaped to the British. Washington himself was one of the discoverers of the plot. Shocked and dismayed, he exclaimed, "Arnold has betrayed us! Whom can we trust now?"

BATTLE OF YORKTOWN

On January 17, 1781, American forces, under the command of Brigadier General Daniel Morgan, clashed with British forces led by Lieutenant Colonel Banastre Tarleton at Cowpens, South Carolina. The Americans scored a total victory through savage fighting. Three months later, Greene and Cornwallis's armies fought a bloody battle at Guilford Courthouse in North Carolina. At the end of the day, the British still held the field, but at a terrible cost of more than five hundred casualties.

Cornwallis then moved on to Wilmington, North Carolina, with his army in tatters. With the main British force out of the way, Greene marched into the heart of South Carolina to regain control of the state. The hard-fought gains the British had made in the south in the last two years were beginning to collapse.

After regrouping in Wilmington, Cornwallis marched his army northward to Virginia, where British forces had been terrorizing the Patriots. Swift and brutal attacks destroyed crops, weapons factories, and other supplies and left many towns in ruins. One of the leaders of these ferocious strike forces was the American traitor, Benedict Arnold.

Washington realized some sort of American response to these attacks was necessary. But he was reluctant to send much of his shrunken army from New

The Articles of Confederation

On March 1, 1781, Maryland became the final colony to ratify (approve) the Articles of Confederation. This document officially set up a federal (national) government for the United States of America. The process of creating and ratifying this document had begun nearly five years earlier, in the summer of 1776. Reaching agreement on the articles had taken a long time and shows that the thirteen states of America were not very strongly united. Each was more interested in protecting its own interests than in protecting the interests of the country as a whole.

The articles gave the national government only limited powers. These included the ability to declare war, to form alliances, and to negotiate peace treaties. The articles also confirmed the Congress's power to coin and borrow money. Yet the states still retained the exclusive power to levy (collect) taxes. Congress could call on the states to supply soldiers and money for the war. But it could do nothing if its requests were not fulfilled. In short, the states still held most of the power. The Congress was forced to continue to finance an expensive war by relying on the individual states to cooperate and support it.

York to Virginia to try to stop the British invasions. The general still believed the key was New York City. If he could take the city back from the British, the war might be won. But Washington did send the Marquis de Lafayette and a small army of 1,200 men to Virginia to try to protect the state. Yet this force was far too small to challenge Cornwallis.

The Marquis de Lafayette

The Marquis de Lafayette (1757–1834) was born into one of the wealthiest families in France. (His full name was Marie-Joseph-Paul-Yves-Roch-Gilbert du Motier de Lafayette.) Although he led a privileged life, Lafayette longed for glory and adventure. At the age of twenty, he purchased a ship and sailed to America to offer his services to the Continental Congress. At first, the congress did not know what to do with this eager young soldier. But when Lafayette volunteered to serve for no pay, he was made a major general. He joined Washington's staff, and the two men became close friends. Lafayette served in several major battles in the war. In addition to his military service, Lafayette also gave money to the American cause. On more than one occasion, he not only paid his own troops but also paid for their uniforms. But perhaps Lafayette's greatest contributions were made during his trips back to France. His clout as one of the country's wealthiest noblemen helped to bring aid for the American cause.

In New York, General Clinton was annoyed when he learned that Cornwallis had left the Carolinas. He ordered Cornwallis to march eastward to Yorktown, Virginia, a port city the army and navy could use as a base of operations.

Yorktown is located next to the York River on a peninsula that juts into the Chesapeake Bay. This long body of water cuts through eastern Virginia and Maryland. Cornwallis and his six thousand troops arrived in Yorktown in early August 1781 and began to set up a defense.

But Cornwallis had put himself in a vulnerable position. He had gathered his forces on the peninsula, with water behind him and a narrow strip of land in front of him. If a strong army approached him on land, his only way to escape would be by water. But if the British navy lost control of the seas surrounding Yorktown, Cornwallis would have only a small area of land through which to escape.

Meanwhile, outside of New York City, Washington received word that a large French fleet, led by Admiral Count de Grasse, was sailing to the Chesapeake to lend assistance to the Americans. Seeing an opportunity to trap Cornwallis's army, Washington quickly abandoned his plans for an invasion of New York.

The American general sent a message to Lafayette to keep Cornwallis confined to Yorktown and made plans to march his army there. Washington's army, joined by Rochambeau's French forces, began their march southward on August 21, 1781. They took indirect routes to mask their intentions from General Clinton in New York. Meanwhile, a second French fleet was setting sail from Newport, Rhode Island, to the Chesapeake. With the addition of Lafayette's small army, already camped near Yorktown, about eighteen thousand soldiers and sailors were moving in on Cornwallis and his six thousand troops.

On August 30, de Grasse's fleet sailed into the Chesapeake and began unloading troops and supplies. On September 5, a British fleet arrived to challenge the French. The ships battled for two hours. The French inflicted heavy damage on the British vessels, which fled to New York. A few days later, the second French fleet arrived from Newport. The French completely controlled

the Chesapeake Bay. Cornwallis could not retreat or be rescued by sea.

On September 28, 1781, the American and French armies marched into the fields and swamps outside of Yorktown. Several days later, the two armies worked under the cover of darkness, digging trenches within range of the British positions. Just like six years earlier before the Battle of Bunker Hill, British commanders woke up to an elaborate network of defensive positions. These trenches were soon filled with thousands of American and French troops and dozens of cannons.

By the afternoon of October 9, the American and French troops and cannons were in place. Washington himself fired the

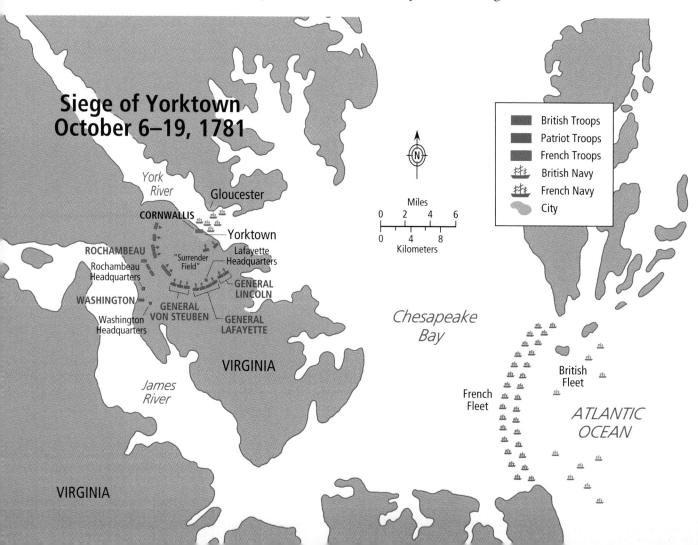

Siege of Yorktown October 6–19, 1781

York River · Gloucester · CORNWALLIS · Yorktown · ROCHAMBEAU · Rochambeau Headquarters · "Surrender Field" · Lafayette Headquarters · GENERAL LINCOLN · WASHINGTON · Washington Headquarters · GENERAL VON STEUBEN · GENERAL LAFAYETTE · VIRGINIA · James River · VIRGINIA

Legend: British Troops · Patriot Troops · French Troops · British Navy · French Navy · City

Miles 0 2 4 6
Kilometers 0 4 8

Chesapeake Bay · French Fleet · British Fleet · ATLANTIC OCEAN

The French victory at the Battle of the Chesapeake Capes cut off Cornwallis's escape from Yorktown.

first cannon shot for the Americans. For three days, they bombarded the British positions. At night, soldiers worked feverishly, digging new and closer trenches.

Cornwallis was running out of food and ammunition. In a letter written to General Clinton on October 15, he described his hopeless situation: "The safety of the place is so precarious [uncertain] that I cannot recommend that the fleet and army should run great risque [risk] in endeavoring [trying] to save us." The general had been expecting reinforcements from New York. Clinton had been preparing to send more than seven thousand men to aid Cornwallis. But it was too late. On October 18, the day before Clinton was to set sail, Cornwallis surrendered.

YORKTOWN SURRENDER CEREMONY

The Yorktown surrender ceremony took place in a large field beyond the battle lines. At 2:00 P.M. on October 19, 1781, Generals Washington and Rochambeau sat upon their horses facing one another. Their troops lined each side of the road leading to Yorktown. The defeated British troops passed between their victors and threw down their weapons in a pile.

As part of the tradition of surrender ceremonies, the

defeated commanding officer was supposed to present his sword to his opponent. But Washington was taken by surprise when General Charles O'Hara, not Cornwallis, rode forward to offer his sword. According to O'Hara, Cornwallis had fallen ill. In fact, Cornwallis was avoiding the humiliating experience of surrendering. He had given his deputy, O'Hara, the miserable task. Washington immediately appointed a deputy of his own. If a deputy was to present the sword of surrender, a deputy would receive it.

Yorktown was the last major battle of the

In this painting of the Yorktown surrender ceremony, Washington's deputy, Benjamin Lincoln *(center, on horse)*, accepts the sword of Cornwallis's deputy, Charles O'Hara *(center, standing)*.

American Revolution. The capture of Cornwallis's army finally convinced Parliament that the war could not be won. Thousands of British lives had been lost, and millions of British pounds had been spent. But the Americans still would not abandon their rebellion. The war had nearly bankrupted the British economy, and many of the country's citizens were opposed to the war.

In early 1782, Parliament had passed a motion that declared, "the war in America be no longer pursued for the impracticable purpose of reducing the inhabitants to obedience by force."

Benjamin Franklin, John Adams, John Jay, and Henry Laurens represented the United States in peace negotiations with the British. One condition of the treaty required Britain to formally recognize the United States of America as an independent nation. The American ambassadors also negotiated new boundaries for the United States. The territory of the new nation extended westward to the Mississippi River, northward to the Great Lakes, and southward to the border of Spanish Florida. (The Native Americans who inhabited much of this land at the time were not consulted. The spread of white Americans onto Indian lands would become a source of conflict well into the future.) The American negotiators also secured the right to fish off the coast of Newfoundland in eastern Canada. The resulting treaty, the Treaty of Paris, was signed on September 3, 1783. The war officially ended on that date. On November 25, 1783, the last British troops sailed out of New York City.

THE HOME FRONT

The Price of Liberty The war brought misery to soldiers and civilians alike. Even Americans living on the home front, away from the fighting, were forced to make sacrifices. They conserved food and faced economic hardships. Men left their farms and businesses to fight, leaving the burdens of home to their families and neighbors.

As her husband leaves for the front, a woman prepares to defend her house.

Quality of life often depended on how close civilians lived to armies. Those who lived far from war zones and army camps suffered fewer hardships than those who were exposed to the war. One of the biggest fears among citizens was having their livestock, crops, and other property taken by the army. This was a common problem, as large armies needed food and other supplies. The practice was discouraged by leaders on both sides, but it was difficult to stop. Lydia M. Post, a Long Island housewife, wrote, "[The Hessian soldiers] take the fence rails to burn, so that the fields are all left open, and the cattle stray away and are often lost."

Support for the war was strong during the early years. But as the conflict dragged on, more and more Americans grew weary of the hardship. Lieutenant Colonel Ebenezer Huntington wrote to his brother from Connecticut in 1779, "This whole part of the Country are Starving for want of bread." Citizens of Prince George County, Virginia, even signed a petition demanding peace with Britain. The document said, "[If] the Sword be not quickly sheathed and Peace restored, [this] land of warfare will sink under the more dreadful effects of griping Penury [severe poverty] and famine."

Patriots vs. Loyalists The revolution wasn't just a war against the British. It was a civil war as well. Conflicts between American Patriots and American Loyalists were not always fought between armies. In cities, towns, and villages across the country, Patriot leaders expected allegiance to the cause of independence. Loyalists who sided with Britain faced persecution—tarring and feathering, loss of property, imprisonment, expulsion, and even execution. But when the British army gained control of an area—such as New York City in 1776 or the southern states later in the war—the tables were turned. Patriots found themselves targets of Loyalists bent on revenge.

In the countryside, these conflicts were often marked by merciless brutality. Members of the two sides waged their own personal wars. Destruction of farms, beatings, and even murder brought the war home to Americans far away from the major battles.

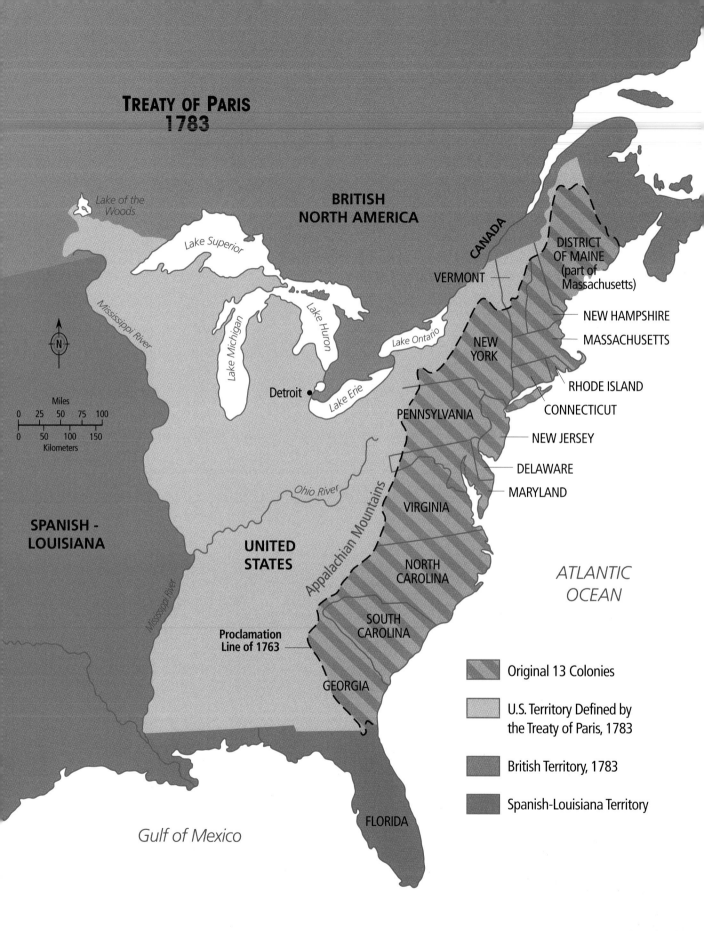

TREATY OF PARIS 1783

Lake of the Woods

BRITISH NORTH AMERICA

CANADA

Lake Superior

Mississippi River

Lake Michigan

Lake Huron

Lake Ontario

Detroit

Lake Erie

Miles
0 25 50 75 100
0 50 100 150
Kilometers

VERMONT

DISTRICT OF MAINE (part of Massachusetts)

NEW HAMPSHIRE

MASSACHUSETTS

NEW YORK

RHODE ISLAND

CONNECTICUT

PENNSYLVANIA

NEW JERSEY

DELAWARE

MARYLAND

Ohio River

Appalachian Mountains

VIRGINIA

SPANISH - LOUISIANA

UNITED STATES

Mississippi River

NORTH CAROLINA

SOUTH CAROLINA

ATLANTIC OCEAN

Proclamation Line of 1763

GEORGIA

Original 13 Colonies

U.S. Territory Defined by the Treaty of Paris, 1783

British Territory, 1783

Spanish-Louisiana Territory

FLORIDA

Gulf of Mexico

CHALLENGES FACING THE NEW NATION

Although the end of the war was cause for celebration, many challenges still lay ahead for the new nation. Major cities such as Charleston and New York City had suffered heavy damage during the fighting. Virtually every tree in New York City had been cut down for firewood during the British occupation. Hard work and hard cash would be needed to rebuild the country.

The fledgling federal government was deeply in debt. Millions were owed to allies such as France, as well as to American merchants and businesspeople who had helped finance the war. But the federal government had no money, nor any power to tax. As before, the federal government had to rely on the states to provide money. Many of the states simply ignored the federal government's calls to help pay the war debt. The scope and limit of the new federal government would become a key issue of debate in the years following the war. The debates would end in the creation and ratification of the Constitution of the United States later in the decade.

These financial difficulties threatened to destroy all that the war had gained. By the spring of 1783, the Continental Army was on the verge of revolt. Angry soldiers and officers were being sent home, but without the pay and pensions they had been promised. The congress owed the army about six million dollars.

In June thousands of angry militiamen marched on Philadelphia and surrounded the congress building, demanding pay and pensions. Washington was forced to call in Continental troops to stop the rebellion. In the end, most of the soldiers and officers who served in the revolution received only about 10 percent of the money the congress had promised them.

Yet despite the overwhelming number of challenges the United States faced, the new nation had the ability to meet them. The country had nearly unlimited natural resources and a hardy, hardworking populace. In years to come, the U.S. government would become the world's first true representative democracy. In a little over a century, it would become the most powerful nation on earth.

MAJOR BATTLES OF THE AMERICAN REVOLUTION

Lexington and Concord, MA	April 19, 1775
Fort Ticonderoga, Canada	May 10, 1775
Crown Point, Canada	May 12, 1775
Bunker Hill, MA	June 17, 1775
Montreal, Canada	November 12, 1775
Quebec, Canada	December 31, 1775
Long Island, NY	August 27, 1776
White Plains, NY	October 28, 1776
Trenton, NJ	December 26, 1776
Princeton, NJ	January 3, 1777
Oriskany, NY	August 6, 1777
Bennington, VT	August 16, 1777
Brandywine, PA	September 11, 1777
Germantown, PA	October 4, 1777
Saratoga, NY	September–October, 1777
Monmouth, NJ	June 28, 1778
Savannah, GA	December 29, 1778
Vincennes (western frontier)	February 24, 1779
Charleston, SC	May 12, 1780
Camden, SC	August 16, 1780
Kings Mountain, SC	October 7, 1780
Cowpens, SC	January 17, 1781
Guilford Courthouse, NC	March 15, 1781
Yorktown, VA	October, 1781

MAJOR BATTLES OF THE AMERICAN REVOLUTION 1775–1781

Lake Superior

Lake Michigan

Lake Huron

Lake Ontario

Lake Erie

Fort Detroit

QUEBEC

Quebec

St. Lawrence River

Montreal

Lake Champlain

Crown Point

Fort Ticonderoga

Saratoga

Oriskany

NEW YORK

NEW HAMPSHIRE

MAINE (part of Massachusetts)

VERMONT (disputed territory)

Bennington

Bunker Hill

Concord

MASSACHUSETTS

Boston

Lexington

West Point

Newport

RHODE ISLAND

CONNECTICUT

White Plains

New York City

Princeton

Germantown

Long Island

Monmouth

PENNSYLVANIA

Valley Forge

Brandywine

Trenton

Philadelphia

NEW JERSEY

DELAWARE

Vincennes

Ohio River

MARYLAND

VIRGINIA

Yorktown

ATLANTIC OCEAN

BRITISH TERRITORIES

Guilford Courthouse

Kings Mountain

NORTH CAROLINA

Cowpens

Wilmington

Camden

N

SOUTH CAROLINA

GEORGIA

Charleston

Savannah

FLORIDA

Gulf of Mexico

	The 13 Colonies
✦	Major Battle
•	City

Miles
0   50   100   150   200

0   100   200   300
Kilometers

AMERICAN REVOLUTION TIMELINE

1763	French and Indian War ends.
	King George III issues the Proclamation Act.
1765	Stamp Act is passed. Colonists protest against it.
1768	British troops arrive in Boston.
1770	Boston Massacre kills five Bostonians on March 5.
1773	On December 16, the Boston Tea Party results in the destruction of British tea.
1774	Parliament passes the Intolerable Acts in response to Boston Tea Party.
	First Continental Congress meets to discuss Intolerable Acts in September.
1775	Minutemen attack British troops at Battles of Lexington and Concord on April 19.
	British suffer heavy casualties at Battle of Bunker Hill on June 17.
1776	*Common Sense* is published in January.
	Declaration of Independence is adopted, July 4.
	New York City falls to the British in September.
	Washington launches surprise attack at Trenton on December 26.
1777	British forces take Philadelphia in September.
	Burgoyne surrenders British army at Saratoga in October.
1778	The United States forms an alliance with France in February.
	British forces seize Savannah in December.
1779	French and Continental forces fail to re-take Savannah in October.
1780	Continental Army routed at Battle of Camden on August 16.
1781	French navy takes control of Chesapeake Bay on September 5.
	Allied forces lay siege to Yorktown, September 28–October 19.
	Cornwallis surrenders British army at Yorktown on October 19.
1783	War ends on September 3 with Treaty of Paris.

GLOSSARY

allies: countries that are fighting for the same cause. France and America were allies in the American Revolution.

campaign: a series of military operations, such as the British invasion of the New York City area

casualty: a military person lost to death, injury, illness, or capture or who is missing in action

customs: taxes or tolls imposed by a country on imports (products) from another country

duty: a tax on imports

empire: a large political unit having power over a large number of territories or peoples. Before independence, the American colonies were part of the British Empire.

enlistment: an agreement to serve in the armed forces. During the early years of the war, Continental Army enlistments were limited to certain periods of time, so it was difficult for General Washington to keep the army together for a long period of time.

ford: a shallow place in a river or waterway where crossing by foot is possible. A ford is an important area in defending a waterway.

laissez-faire: roughly translated from the French as "free to do;" a philosophy followed by the British government that sought as little governmental interference in economic affairs as possible

mercenary: a soldier hired to serve in the army of a foreign country

militia: a group of citizens organized for military service. Militiamen fought alongside the professional Continental Army in many battles during the revolution.

morale: the state of the spirits of an individual or a group as shown by their willingness to do assigned tasks

propaganda: the spreading of information or publicity to promote or oppose a policy, idea, doctrine, or cause. Often propaganda can be deceptive or distorted in its presentation.

reinforcements: in military terms, fresh troops that can add to or replace troops fighting on the front line

resolution: a statement that is adopted by a governing body or a group and that clearly states what that body or group resolves (plans) to do

siege: the surrounding or blockading of a town or fortress by an army or navy with the intention of capturing the town or fortress

WHO'S WHO?

John Adams (1735–1826)

Adams was born in Braintree, Massachusetts, and became a leader of American opposition to British colonial rule in 1765. He was elected to the Continental Congress in 1774, where he slowly began to favor American independence. Adams championed the Declaration of Independence in 1776 and helped to persuade the congress to ratify it. He served under George Washington as the first vice president of the United States. He was elected the country's second president in 1796.

John Burgoyne (1722–1792)

Known as Gentleman Johnny, Burgoyne entered the British army in 1740 and later became a major general. In June 1777, he successfully recaptured Fort Ticonderoga. Later that summer, he and his army were defeated in battle near Saratoga, New York. Burgoyne and his army were forced to surrender to General Horatio Gates. The defeat inspired France to agree to an alliance with America.

Charles Cornwallis (1738–1805)

Cornwallis, born in London, was promoted to major general in the British army in 1775. A shrewd and aggressive military leader, he was a key contributor to the Battle of Brandywine Creek. In 1780 he became a commander of British forces in the south. Cornwallis was victorious at Camden in 1780 but was trapped by American and French forces at Yorktown in 1781. His defeat ended the major fighting of the war.

Horatio Gates (1728–1806)

A former soldier in the British army, Gates was born in England. He retired from the British army in 1765 and lived on a farm in Virginia. In 1775 Gates was recruited by Washington to be a brigadier general. By 1776 he was a major general serving in the north. Later in the war, he led forces in the south and was replaced by Nathanael Greene after fleeing the battlefield at Camden.

Nathanael Greene (1742–1786)

Greene was born in Warwick, Rhode Island, and became the army's youngest brigadier general in 1775. After serving at the siege of Boston, he was promoted to major general and was given command of the New Jersey army. He served at Trenton, New Jersey, as well as at the Battles of Brandywine Creek and Germantown, Pennsylvania. In 1780 he was appointed by Washington to command the south. He successfully limited British control of the south.

Thomas Jefferson (1743–1826)

Born in Albemarle County, Virginia, Jefferson was elected to the Continental Congress in 1775. He was appointed to the committee to draft the Declaration of Independence in 1776. His skill as a writer made him the logical choice to draft the document. He became governor of Virginia in 1779 and a minister to France in 1785. In 1800 Jefferson was elected the third president of the United States.

Henry Knox (1750–1806)

A self-taught soldier and close friend of George Washington, Knox was born in Boston. He served as a volunteer in the Boston militia when the revolution began but was soon appointed by Washington as a commander of artillery. Knox coordinated and led the transport of British cannons from Fort Ticonderoga, New York, to Boston during the winter of 1775–1776. He was promoted to brigadier general after his service in the Battle of Trenton and became a major general in 1782. Knox succeeded Washington as commander in chief in 1783.

Count de Rochambeau (1725–1807)

A French aristocrat, Rochambeau served with his country's army in the War of Austrian Succession (1740–1748) and the Seven Years' War (1754–1763). In 1780 he was promoted to lieutenant general and sent to America with French forces. He formed a good relationship with Washington. Together they created war plans for the French and American alliance. Rochambeau's army combined with Washington's at Yorktown, leading to Cornwallis's surrender.

Baron Friedrich Wilhelm von Steuben (1730–1794)

Born in Prussia (part of modern-day Germany), von Steuben met Benjamin Franklin in Paris and volunteered for the Patriots. At the Continental Army camp at Valley Forge in the winter of 1777-1778, he showed his value as a drillmaster, teaching soldiers the value of discipline. He was appointed inspector general to the Continental Army. Von Steuben later wrote the first-ever American army manual of drills and regulations.

SOURCE NOTES

9   Benson Bobrick, *Angel in the Whirlwind.* (New York: Simon & Schuster, 1997), 29.

15   Mark M. Boatner, III, *Encyclopedia of the American Revolution* (Mechanicsburg, PA: Stackpole Books,1994), 94.

16   John Anthony Scott, *The Story of the American Revolution. A National Geographic Picture Atlas* (Washington, D.C.: The National Geographic Society, 1984), 71.

17   Milton Meltzer, ed., *The American Revolutionaries: A History in Their Own Words, 1750–1800* (New York: Thomas Y. Crowell, 1987), 51.

20   Henry Steele Commager, and Richard B. Morris, eds., *The Spirit of Seventy-Six: The Story of the American Revolution as Told by Participants* (New York: Da Capo Press, Inc.,1995), 81–82.

22   Thomas Fleming, *Liberty! The American Revolution* (New York: Viking, 1997), 88.

22   Don Higginbotham, *The War of American Independence* (New York: The MacMillan Company, 1972), 125.

23   George F. Scheer, ed., *Rebels & Redcoats: The American Revolution Through the Eyes of Those Who Fought and Lived It* (New York: Da Capo Press, Inc., unabridged republication of 1957 edition by the World Publishing Company), 35.

26   R. G. Grant, *Revolution! The American Revolution* (New York: Thomson Learning, 1995), 18.

26   Russell B. Adams, Jr., ed., *The American Story: The Revolutionaries, 1775–1783* (Alexandria, VA: Time-Life Books, 1996), 53.

28   Fleming, *Liberty!,* 142.

31   Ibid., 150.

31   Harry M. Ward, *The American Revolution: Nationhood Achieved, 1763–1788* (New York: St. Martin's Press, 1995), 201.

31   Ibid., 202.

31   Ibid.

34   Esmond Wright, *The Fire of Liberty* (New York: St. Martin's Press, 1983), 78.

36   Commager and Morris, eds., *The Spirit of Seventy-Six,* 302.

38   Dumas Malone, *The Story of the Declaration of Independence* (New York: Oxford University Press, 1954), 3–4.

44   Fleming, *Liberty!,* 202.

45   Richard Brookhiser, *Founding Father* (New York: The Free Press, 1996), 26.

46   Rupert Furneaux, *The Pictorial History of the American Revolution as Told by Eyewitnesses and Participants* (Chicago: J. G. Ferguson Publishing Company, 1973), 141.

47   Adams, Jr., ed., *The American Story: The Revolutionaries, 1775–1783,* 93.

48   John Rhodehamel, ed., *The American Revolution: Writings from the War of Independence* (New York: The Library of America, 2001), 260–261.

50   Scheer, ed. *Rebels & Redcoats,* 264.

51   W. J. Wood, *Battles of the Revolutionary War, 1775–1781* (New York: Da Capo Press, 1995), 110.

57   Bobrick, *Angel in the Whirlwind,* 287.

59   Joy Hakim, *From Colonies to Country* (New York: Oxford University Press, 1993), 128.

59   Boatner, *Encyclopedia of the American Revolution,* 725.

60   Fleming, *Liberty!,* 288.

65   C. Keith Wilbur, *Revolutionary Medicine, 1700–1800* (Philadelphia, PA: Chelsea House Publishers, 1980), 9.

68   Ray Raphael, *A People's History of the American Revolution* (New York: The New Press, 2001), 82.

70   Fleming, *Liberty!,* 311.

73   Christopher Hibbert, *Redcoats and Rebels: The American Revolution through British Eyes* (New York: Avon Books, 1990), 328.

73   John Tebbel, *Turning the World Upside Down* (New York: Orion Books, 1993), 397.

73   Fleming, *Liberty!,* 336.

75   Ward, *The American Revolution,* 199.

75   Ibid., 198.

SELECTED BIBLIOGRAPHY, FURTHER READING, AND WEBSITES

SELECTED BIBLIOGRAPHY

Adams, Jr., Russell B., ed. *The American Story: The Revolutionaries, 1775–1783*. Alexandria, VA: Time-Life Books, 1996.

Barnes, Ian. *The Historical Atlas of the American Revolution*. New York: Routledge, 2000.

Boatner, III, Mark M. *Encyclopedia of the American Revolution*. Mechanicsburg, PA: Stackpole Books, 1994.

Burg, David F. *The American Revolution: An Eyewitness History*. New York: Facts-on-File, Inc., 2001.

Canon, Jill. *Heroines of the American Revolution*. Santa Barbara, CA: Bellerophon Books, 1998.

Commager, Henry Steele, and Richard B. Morris, eds. *The Spirit of Seventy-Six: The Story of the American Revolution as Told by Participants*. New York: Da Capo Press, Inc.,1995.

Davis, Burke. *Black Heroes of the American Revolution*. New York: Harcourt Brace Jovanovich, Publishers, 1976.

Fleming, Thomas. *Liberty! The American Revolution*. New York: Viking, 1997.

Hakim, Joy. *From Colonies to Country*. New York: Oxford University Press, 1993.

Raphael, Ray. *A People's History of the American Revolution*. New York: The New Press, 2001.

Rhodehamel, John, ed. *The American Revolution: Writings from the War of Independence*. New York: The Library of America, 2001.

Ward, Harry M. *The American Revolution: Nationhood Achieved, 1763–1788*. New York: St. Martin's Press, 1995.

FURTHER READING

Behrman, Carol. *John Adams*. Minneapolis, MN: Lerner Publications Company, 2004.

Canon, Jill. *Heroines of the American Revolution*. Santa Barbara, CA: Bellerophon Books, 1998.

Collier, Christopher, and James Lincoln Collier. *The Drama of American History: The American Revolution 1763–1783*. New York: Benchmark Books, 1998.

Day, Nancy. *Your Travel Guide to Colonial America*. Minneapolis, MN: Runestone Press, 2001.

Dolan, Edward F. *The American Revolution: How We Fought the War of Independence*. Brookfield, CT: The Millbrook Press, 1995.

Ferris, Jerry. *Thomas Jefferson: Father of Liberty*. Minneapolis, MN: Carolrhoda Books, Inc., 1998.

Fritz, John. *Why Not, Lafayette?* New York: G. P. Putnam's Sons, 1999.

Furbee, Mary R. *Women of the American Revolution*. San Diego, CA: Lucent Books, 1999.

Miller, Brandon Marie. *Growing Up in Revolution and the New Nation, 1775 to 1800*. Minneapolis, MN: Lerner Publications Company, 2003.

Nardo, Don. *The Declaration of Independence: A Model for Individual Rights*. San Diego, CA: Lucent Books, 1999.

Roberts, Jeremy. *George Washington*. Minneapolis, MN: Lerner Publications Company, 2004.

Streissguth, Tom. *Benjamin Franklin*. Minneapolis, MN: Lerner Publications Company, 2002.

Swain, Gwenyth. *Declaring Freedom: A Look at the Declaration of Independence, the Bill of Rights, and the Constitution*. Minneapolis, MN: Lerner Publications Company, 2004.

Weber, Michael. *The Making of America: The American Revolution*. New York: Raintree Steck-Vaughn, 2000.

WEBSITES

Benjamin Franklin. Learn more about this amazing American legend.
<http://www.pbs.org/benfranklin/>

Guilford Courthouse National Military Park. Visit the online exhibits from Guilford Courthouse, North Carolina, site of one of the key battles of the American Revolution.
<http://www.cr.nps.gov/museum/exhibits/revwar/guco/gucooverview.html>

Independence National Historical Park. Visit the online exhibits from this national park in Philadelphia. The site includes portraits of many of the Continental Army's generals.
<http://www.cr.nps.gov/museum/exhibits/revwar/inde/indeoverview.html>

Liberty! The American Revolution. This is the companion website to the PBS documentary mini-series.
<http://www.pbs.org/ktca/liberty/>

Valley Forge National Historical Park. Visit the online exhibits of the site of the Continental Army's miserable winter encampment of 1777–1778 at Valley Forge, Pennsylvania.
<http://www.cr.nps.gov/museum/exhibits/revwar/vafo/vafooverview.html>

INDEX

Laurens, Henry, 74
lawmaking, 7, 31
Lee, Arthur, 56
Lee, Richard Henry, 36–37
legislatures, colonial, 7, 10, 11
Lexington and Concord, Battles of, 19–21, 23
Liberty Bell, 38
Lincoln, Benjamin, 67, 74
Long Island, Battle of, 39–40; map, 41
Loyalists, 32–33, 65–67, 68, 75

Manhattan Island, 39, 42
maps, 8, 27, 41, 72, 76, 79
medical conditions, 57–58, 62–63
mercenaries, 37, 39, 45, 46, 49
Midnight Riders, 19, 20
militias, 18, 19, 20, 54
minutemen, 18, 20–21
Monmouth, Battle of, 59–60
Montreal, 32
Morgan, Daniel, 54

Native Americans, 9, 30, 60, 74
Navigation Acts, 7
navy, American, 59, 64–65
navy, British, 18, 26, 33, 39, 59, 64–65, 66, 72
navy, French, 59, 66, 71–73
neutrality, 33
New France, 8, 9
New York City, 4, 12, 36, 39, 40, 41, 67, 70, 76;
    British occupation of, 42, 43, 75
North, Lord, 22

Paine, Thomas, 33–34
Parliament, 7, 10–11, 12, 14, 16, 17, 19, 22, 33;
    declares end of war, 73–74
Patriots, 14–16, 75
peace negotiations, 74
Philadelphia, Pennsylvania, 18, 50–51, 54, 59, 76
Pitcher, Molly, 60
Pitt, William, 22
Prescott, William, 26
Princeton, New Jersey, 48
privateers, 64–65
Proclamation of Rebellion, 29
Proclamation of 1763, 9, 60; map, 76
Prohibitory Act, 33

Quartering Act, 10
Quebec, 32

Revenue Act of 1764 (Sugar Act), 10
Revere, Paul, 15–16, 19, 20
Rochambeau, Count de, 69, 73, 83
Rush, Benjamin, 31

Sampson, Deborah, 31
Saratoga, Battle of, 54–56, 67
Savannah, Georgia, 66–67
scorched-earth tactics, 42, 49
Serapis, 64–65
Sessions, Robert, 17
Seven Years' War, 9
slavery, 30, 32
smuggling, 7, 16
social classes, 44, 45, 52
soldiers, American 4, 5, 39, 44, 62, 69, 76
soldiers, British, 9, 39, 45
Sons of Liberty, 11, 15, 17
southern colonies, 32
southern states, war in, 65–68, 70, 75
spies, 40, 43, 46
Stamp Act, 10–12, 25
Stamp Act Congress, 12
Steuben, Friedrich Wilhelm von, 58–59, 83

Tarleton, Banastre, 70, 70, 83
tarring and feathering, 12, 75
taxation without representation, 10–11, 12
taxes: by federal government, 76; by Parliament, 7,
    10–13, 16, 17, 22, 28
Tea Act, 16–17
Ticonderoga, Fort, 24, 35, 39, 43, 49, 54
Townshend Acts, 13, 16
trade between America and Britain, 6–7, 12, 22
trade laws, 7, 25
Treaty of Paris, 74; map of, 77
Trenton, New Jersey, 4, 5; Battle of, 46–47

uniforms, 44–45
United States of America, 74; Constitution of the,
    76; map, 77
unity of colonies, 12–13, 18, 23
unity of states, 70, 76

Valley Forge, 57–59
Vincennes, 61, 64
violence: civilian, 11, 15,19, 68, 75; frontier, 60–61
voting rights, 7

Washington, George, 4, 18, 25, 28–29, 36, 39,
    41–43, 46–47, 57, 59, 67, 69, 70, 71, 76
weapons, 19, 24, 44, 52–53; transportation of, 5, 35, 50
West Indies, 6, 30, 45
winter encampments, 43, 49, 57–58
women, 30, 31, 60

Yorktown: Battle of, 70–74; map, 72; surrender at,
    73–74

ABOUT THE AUTHOR

Lisa Frederiksen Bohannon has published two biographies and several articles on career planning and management. Bohannon earned a degree in economics from the University of California at Davis and worked for twenty-three years in the field of executive management before retiring to devote her time to raising her children and writing. She lives in Menlo Park, California, with her husband and their six children.

PHOTO ACKNOWLEDGMENTS

The images in this book are used with the permission of: Library of Congress, pp. 4–5 [LC-D416-550], 11 (bottom) [LC-USZ62-115162], 12 [LC-USZ62-138], 16 (bottom) [LC-USZC4-4600], 17 [LC-USZC4-523], 21 [LC-USZ62-8623], 25 [LC-USZ62-39570], 34 [LC-USZ62-31982-216D], 51 [LC-USZ62-100726], 58 (bottom), 61, 71 [LC-USZC4-4526], 83 (third from top) [LC-USZ62-11396]; © North Wind Picture Archives, pp. 6, 7, 9, 10, 11 (top), 13, 15, 18 (both), 19, 20, 22, 23, 24, 26, 28, 29, 30 (both), 31, 33 (top), 37 (both), 38, 40, 47 (both), 48, 49, 54, 55, 58 (top), 66, 67, 69, 73, 75, 82 (second and third from top), 83 (bottom); © Independent Picture Service, pp. 14, 33, 36 (both), 59, 65, 68, 82 (fourth from top), 83 (second from top), 83 (third from top); National Archives, pp. 16 (top) [148-CD-4-15], 39 [W&C #70], 46 [W&C #31], 57 [W&C #36], 60 [W&C #37], 82 (top) [148-CD-4-15]; General Research Division, New York Public Library, p. 32; Delaware Public Archives, p. 35; Courtesy of the Brooklyn Historical Society, p. 42; The Connecticut Historical Society, p. 43; National Parks Service, pp. 44, 45, 52–53 (all), 62, 63 (top); White House Collection, p. 56; Courtesy of the Bakken Museum Department of Special Collections, p. 63 (bottom); Naval Academy Museum, p. 64; Yale University Art Gallery, p. 74; Independence National Historical Park Collection, p. 82 (bottom). Maps by Laura Westlund, pp. 9, 27, 41, 72, 77, 79.

Cover image by Peter Newark's American Pictures.